# CARPAL TUNNEL SYNDROME AND OTHER REPETITIVE STRAIN INJURIES

—Diseases and People—

# CARPAL TUNNEL SYNDROME AND OTHER REPETITIVE STRAIN INJURIES

Philip Johansson

**Enslow Publishers, Inc.**

40 Industrial Road          PO Box 38
Box 398                     Aldershot
Berkeley Heights, NJ 07922  Hants GU12 6BP
USA                         UK

http://www.enslow.com

**Library of Congress Cataloging-in-Publication Data**

Johansson, Philip.
    Carpal tunnel syndrome and other repetitive strain injuries / Philip Johansson.
      p. cm.—(Diseases and people)
    Includes bibliographical references and index.
    Summary: Examines repetitive strain injuries such as carpal tunnel syndrome, tennis
elbow, and tendinitis, their causes, symptoms, diagnosis, treatment, and prevention.
    ISBN 0-7660-1184-4
    1. Overuse injuries—Juvenile literature. 2. Carpal tunnel syndrome—Juvenile
literature. [1. Overuse injuries.] I. Title. II. Series.
RD97.6.J64   1999
616.8'7—dc21                     98-30305
                                             CIP
                                             AC

**To Our Readers:**
All Internet addresses in this book were active and appropriate when we went to press. Any
comments or suggestions can be sent by e-mail to Comments@enslow.com or to the address
on the back cover.

**Illustration Credits:** Joan Carey, pp. 25, 38; Philip Johansson, pp. 12, 17, 29, 33,
42, 45, 54, 55, 61, 67, 70, 72, 78, 85, 88, 98.

**Cover Illustration:** © Corel Corporation.

# Contents

# Acknowledgments

The author expresses his sincere gratitude to Dr. Jody E. Noé, Brad Hurley, and Joan Carey for their careful reading of the manuscript and their many helpful comments. Many thanks also to Louisa Mann and Jon Lauden, at The Neighborhood Schoolhouse, for taking the time to read and comment on it. I am grateful to my many photogenic subjects, for allowing their photographs to appear in this book, and to Jane, for the story of her experience with RSI. This book is dedicated to Allie, who also knows what it feels like.

# CARPAL TUNNEL SYNDROME AND OTHER REPETITIVE STRAIN INJURIES

**What is it?** A group of physical ailments of muscles, tendons, and nerves that result from repeated motions performed over a long time.

**Who gets it?** Anyone can, but most often adults who use repetitive motions in their work or recreation.

**How do you get it?** Repetitive strain injuries develop gradually, after months or years of performing the same motions over and over. Usually the repetitive motions are accompanied by poor posture, inappropriate positioning, poorly designed tools or workstations, stress, or other related factors.

**What are the symptoms?** Numbness, tingling, pain, or loss of strength usually in the hand, wrist, arm, shoulder, or neck. Many people ignore the first signs of tingling or numbness, which leads to more severe and serious symptoms that can signal irreversible damage. Some people first experience symptoms while they are performing their usual repetitive motion, such as hammering or typing. Others first notice symptoms when performing unrelated motions, like opening a jar.

**How is it treated?** If caught early enough, a program of rest, gradual rehabilitation, and reconditioning of the affected part can resolve the symptoms. More serious cases are treated with splints, drugs that reduce inflammation, or even surgery.

**How is it prevented?** People who regularly perform repetitive motions must learn how to do them with proper posture and positioning. Short breaks, stretches, and conditioning exercises can also help avoid repetitive strain injuries.

# 1

# The Disease of Monotony

lara was an aspiring poet and novelist, as well as a full-time aide to a college president. After spending a long day at work, she would hurry home and eagerly respond to her daily e-mail and add to her latest novel. Her hands were like wildfire on the keyboard. She hustled her mouse around its mouse pad, clenching it with white knuckles as if it were the doorknob to her future. Clara's writing career was starting to take off, and she was eager to get on with it. It never occurred to her that she could have too much of a good thing.

It started with twinges in her neck and right shoulder. Then her right wrist started hurting. Clara tried using the mouse with her left hand instead, and she began to have the same symptoms on her left side. She had to give up swing dancing because it hurt too much to hold her partner's hand.

Then she finally had to quit her job because she could no longer hold the strap on the bus to work. Friends had to help her do her chores and buy her groceries. At the age of thirty-one, Clara had to pamper her arms like a woman three times her age racked by arthritis. Due to her hours of diligent work, she suffered from the disease of monotony: repetitive strain injury.[1]

Repetitive strain injury (RSI) results when muscles, tendons, or neighboring parts of the body become damaged from prolonged overuse, repetitive use, improper use, or a combination of these. Unlike broken bones or torn cartilage, RSI does not require a car accident, football injury, or other grisly trauma. It works quietly and unexpectedly, resulting from repetitive motions as seemingly innocent as throwing a ball, tightening screws, or, in Clara's case, working at a computer. Pain, weakness, numbness, or loss of control—even permanent disability—can result if not corrected.

Your body is a massive network of muscles and tendons that moves your bones around so that you can dance, fly a kite, or eat a sandwich. The muscles do the contracting, and the tendons that connect the muscles to bones transfer that movement to the bones. RSI can conceivably happen anywhere in this network, and it comes in different shapes and sizes. However, it is most commonly reported in people's hands, arms, shoulders, and necks and frequently results from the kind of work or sport they do. RSIs with names like golfer's elbow or writer's cramp suggest that the repetitive nature of some activities can be dangerous.

RSI is a grab bag of several related injuries that also collectively go by other names. They have been called wear-and-tear disorders, overuse injuries, cumulative trauma disorders, repetitive motion injuries, repetitive motion syndromes, repetitive strain disorders, and many other things.[2] For the sake of simplicity, they will all be referred to in this book as repetitive strain injuries. The most widely known RSI is carpal tunnel syndrome, a debilitating disorder of the wrist. Carpal tunnel syndrome is actually rare among RSIs, amounting to only 10 percent of all tendon-related disorders.[3] Although carpal tunnel syndrome is often thought to be equivalent to RSI, there are many other examples of RSI that deserve equal attention.

Clara now warns friends to treat their computers "like a chainsaw, because you could lose an arm to it."[4] But computer users are not the only people at risk for RSI. They share similar repetitive motions with travel agents and pianists, who all sit

# Agonists and Antagonists

Most muscles work in pairs in order to make bones move. The muscles on one side, the agonists, shorten, while those on the other side, the antagonists, lengthen. The strength and coordination of bodily movements rely on the cooperation of these pairs. Any impediment to this interaction, such as tight or fatigued muscles, makes them more vulnerable to injury.

for hours and tap repetitively with their fingers. Carpenters, taxi drivers, domestic workers, assembly workers, surgeons, needleworkers, and architects put different strains on their bodies, but these strains can all lead to injury if people do not take proper precautions.

More than half the nation's workers have jobs with RSI potential.[5] RSI accounts for 60 percent of all job-related injuries, costing businesses billions of dollars a year in disability compensation.[6] RSI knows no boundaries of age, class, or education. Stephanie Barnes, founder of the Association for Repetitive Motion Syndromes, reports RSIs in "artists, blacksmiths, hairdressers, massage therapists and people in dozens

Our hands are miracles in natural engineering, adapted for the finest of movements and the firmest of grips. But they do have their limits.

of other professions. It's an epidemic."[7] Wherever there is repetition, there can be an RSI.

But it does not have to be this way. Repetition by itself does not cause RSI: It must be accompanied by poor posture and positioning, improper muscle conditioning, lack of flexibility, and ill-fitting workstation design or other negative working conditions. Work-related stress or other psychological factors can also contribute to the problem. In order to reduce the incidence of RSI in the workplace and beyond, people must become more aware of the risks involved with repetitive motions and how to avoid them.

Clara may have to deal with a lifetime of discomfort and disability from her fervent computer use, but there is still hope for the rest of us. Whether you are a fisherman, bowler, student, carpenter, butcher, baker, or candlestick maker, the future of RSI is in your hands—and in how effectively and carefully you use them.

# 2

# Birth of an Illness

In the early 1700s an Italian doctor, Bernardino Ramazzini, made note of certain workplace hazards that had nothing to do with dangerous machines or materials. He noticed "certain violent and irregular motions and unnatural positions of the body, by reason of which the natural structure of the vital machine is so impaired that serious diseases gradually develop from them."[1] He also pointed out that even healthful and harmless exercises that people did for recreation could lead to serious disorders if they were overdone.[2] The diseases that Ramazzini was talking about were RSIs, but it would take over two hundred years before the implications of his findings were appreciated.

Repetitive strain injury is nothing new, but it has only received widespread attention in the last decade. It was not even given this name until the 1980s. There are no statistics of

RSI through the ages, but its legacy is found in the names of disorders associated with certain trades, such as bricklayer's shoulder, carpenter's elbow, stitcher's wrist, gamekeeper's thumb, and cotton-twister's hand.[3] Telegraphers from as early as the mid-nineteenth century were suffering from telegrapher's cramp, the result of tapping messages out at a rate of thousands of taps a day. Every manual trade had its RSI, from meat packers to milkers.

Historically, these maladies were shrugged off as the result of overuse and old age, and no connection was made between them. The physical changes underlying them were not well understood and were not considered as critical as traumatic injuries, infectious diseases, or other medically noteworthy ailments. They were just the everyday aches and pains that one would expect from working hard for a living. Typically, the people who performed manual labor were at the highest risk for RSI, although musicians, writers, and telegraphers are notable exceptions.

## The Modern Age of RSI

Repetitive strain injury has always been with us, but the growing epidemic has its roots in the industrial revolution of the early 1800s. The risks of manual labor were magnified by the introduction of machines used in factories, because workers were required to do more repetitive tasks at a quicker pace. For instance, some modern assembly-line workers do the same motion—whether it is turning a screw, snapping on a cap, or merely pushing a button—more than twenty-five thousand times in one day.[4] Machines lighten the workload and distribute it evenly among workers, but they also increase the pace and require concentrated use of weaker body parts such as hands and wrists. These parts are more vulnerable to RSI, especially in the modern mechanized workplace.

If industrialization began the RSI snowball rolling, the high-technology revolution has caused an avalanche. In 1981 the first personal computer was released, and just a decade later RSI was one of the fastest growing problems facing American businesses.[5] Computer users are the largest single occupational group ever, and they are showing up with RSIs in record numbers. Seventy million Americans, including children,

Expansion of computer use has paralleled the increase in RSI cases.

spend part of their day at a computer.[6] Three quarters of all jobs require the use of a computer. Without measures toward safer computer use, RSI could become the wave of the future.

Not only are computers everywhere, they are extremely well suited as a potential cause for RSI. Users spend long hours doing nothing but sitting and repeatedly flicking their fingers to beat the speed of the latest microchip. It may not seem like much to complain about, since each keystroke requires a tiny 1.5 ounces of pressure. But this adds up to over a ton in a day's worth of typing, and thousands of repetitions without any break. Although they may think nothing of it, computer users are running up against the real limits of the human body. Many people have bad typing techniques that put pressure on their wrists and fingers, the weakest parts of their bodies. In the wrong hands, a computer keyboard can be a dangerous weapon.

One would think that computer-related RSI had its predecessor in the old manual typewriters, which required far more force for each keystroke. But these two machines are as different as apples and oranges. Typewriters would allow a typist to go only so fast before the type bars (mechanical arms that imprinted each letter) would jam. Computer keyboards, on the other hand, challenge the fastest typing skills. Typewriters also required related tasks, like loading paper, pushing the return bar, or correcting errors. These enforced rests added variety to the typist's motions. The keys on typewriters were stepped so that typists had to support their arms with their upper bodies, using the stronger muscles of their shoulders and upper arms, rather than resting their wrists on the desk.

There may have been rare cases of RSI among typists who used the old mechanical typewriters, but for computer users, it comes with the territory. With no paper to load, no return bar to push, and no type bars to untangle, the computer keyboard is streamlined for repetitive motion. RSI cases in computer-intensive industries went up forty-two-fold between 1985 and 1994.[7] Up to one quarter of all computer users have some symptoms of RSI.[8]

## Today's Aches and Pains

Are modern-day RSI sufferers just more wimpy than their predecessors? Do they just complain louder about the everyday aches and pains that one can expect from a hard day's work? Even now, doctors may not give RSI victims the full attention they deserve because they may not completely understand its complexity or even believe in its reality.[9] Current understanding has certainly allowed more and more sufferers to step forward and have their painful and perplexing symptoms acknowledged and relieved. But greater awareness about RSI cannot begin to explain the current epidemic we are in.

In 1985, the National Institute for Occupational Safety and Health proposed a national strategy for preventing musculoskeletal injuries, namely RSI. In their report they identified research and information needs and pointed out how jobs could be changed to make them safer for employees.[10] Some companies have responded to these suggestions,

# The Cost of Healing[11]

The average compensation for rehabilitating work-related RSI is $29,000 per victim. These injuries are costing businesses billions of dollars.

but the necessary changes can cost a lot of money. Making a workplace RSI-free requires investing in better chairs, workstation modifications, enforced breaks in production, consultants in occupational therapy and workstation design, and other costly measures. But at the current rate of rise in RSI complaints, it will only be a matter of time before employers realize that making jobs safer is more cost-effective in the long run.

# 3

# The Slowest Injury

Jane worked in a school cafeteria, preparing food for hundreds of hungry children and cleaning up after them. It did not seem like a dangerous job to her. It was not like building skyscrapers or cutting down huge trees, but Jane's body knew that the cafeteria was a hotbed of repetitive perils. Every day she stirred thick sauces, lifted heavy pots and pans, and opened heavy cans with a giant, prehistoric can opener. Washing dishes required squeezing a spray nozzle for countless minutes, continuously straining the muscles in her forearm and hand.

After only a year at the cafeteria, Jane began noticing that her hands would always fall asleep at night. She could not find a position in bed to prevent this, though she tried everything. Soon she experienced pains in her whole forearm and numbness in her hand. She would even get shooting pains between

21

her fingers. To lift a milk carton with her right hand, she needed to support her wrist with the left one. Everything took two hands, from carrying groceries to opening doors. She could not even tuck blankets in under her children's beds.

The last straw was when the garbage disposal at the cafeteria broke. Instead of being able to let the water from washing dishes go down the drain, Jane had to fill ten-gallon buckets with the dirty water and pour them into a drain in the kitchen floor. The heavy buckets took their toll on Jane's already injured arms. She experienced her worst pains yet and took two weeks off from work to recover from the strain. Her doctor diagnosed Jane with carpal tunnel syndrome and gave her a shot of cortisone, which hurt almost as much as carrying the ten-gallon bucket. Building skyscrapers or cutting down huge trees would have been a piece of cake compared to this.[1]

## Symptoms: What RSI Feels Like

The symptoms of RSI are sneaky. There are as many combinations of symptoms as there are people who have them. Many people are unaware of any symptoms at first. Others feel excruciating pain that burns, aches, or shoots from the site of injury and that typically involves any part of the body from the hand to the neck. Sometimes just the *thought* of doing the repetitive motion that caused the injury is enough to bring on pain. Other symptoms can include weakness of the hand or arm, fatigue, tingling, numbness, heaviness, clumsiness, stiffness, or hypersensitivity.

People with RSI often first notice symptoms away from work or the repetitive motion that caused the injury. They may find that they have difficulty opening doors, or they lose their grip on the book they are reading. It may be painful to wash the dishes. Their hand tingles when they brush their hair or becomes achy and tired from holding the garden hose. In Jane's case it was painful to pour milk. Symptoms might occur only when certain actions are performed, be chronic all day, or worsen at night. Many symptoms may disappear altogether or move to a different spot if the person changes his or her position or posture. This slippery character of RSI symptoms leads many victims, even some doctors, to disregard them.

Often one of the first symptoms to alert people that they have an injury is how they modify their own behavior. They may avoid using one of their hands for things like turning on a light. They may use other body parts to perform actions, like their shoulder for opening doors. They may change sports, from tennis to soccer. They might shop for food more often so that they have smaller bags to carry. They might buy less food that they have to peel or chop. They might even avoid certain clothes in their closet because they are hard to button. Some people feel the first twinges of pain when they shake someone's hand in greeting. Whether people respond to these first hints of symptoms can mean the difference between recovery and lifelong debilitation.

RSI symptoms can be confusing because they involve connective tissues. The connective tissues, including blood, bone, cartilage, tendons, and ligaments, hold the body together and have no beginning and no end. So an injury in one area can travel to another, transmitted through the body like a signal. A stiff neck can result in shoulder pain, which can result in weakness of the hands.

A person may not even feel pain at the point of injury but find it somewhere else instead. This "referred pain" often follows patterns based on areas of the body called dermatomes. Each dermatome originates from one of the original thirty-two segments that make up the human embryo. For instance, the shoulder and the upper arm are in the same dermatome, and someone with RSI in her shoulder may not feel any shoulder pain but instead have pain in her upper arm.[2]

This perplexing assortment of aches, pains, and numbness that make up the symptoms of RSI have been known for centuries as carpenter's elbow, stitcher's wrist, and various other names. But the exact physical causes for these symptoms have been revealed only in the past few decades. These causes are the basis for grouping such a diverse set of ailments under the name RSI.

## Physical Causes

For bones to move relative to each other—for instance, for an elbow to bend—the muscles on one side must contract while the ones on the other side relax and lengthen. Tendons are tough, fibrous tissues like ropes that connect muscles to bones and transfer the actions of muscles to the movement of bones. A person's strength and coordination depends on the ability of

Activities that people have done for centuries, such as splitting wood, can contribute to RSI.

his muscles to both contract and relax. The tendons also need to transfer these actions smoothly. An injury to the musculoskeletal system, such as a strain, interferes with the smooth and balanced workings of muscles and tendons. Normally the tissues can heal well if given enough time. But in the case of RSI, damage to the muscles and tendons that are relied on for work or pleasure proceeds faster than the natural healing process can keep up with.

Many risk factors can be instrumental in the physical changes that accompany RSI, but damage to a muscle or tendon is the greatest single risk factor. Muscle strain, from repetitive motion or from an acute injury, results in microscopic tears in the muscle fibers. The fibers become inflamed and swollen and accumulate waste products and debris. They also stick to neighboring tissues like glue, a problem called adhesion. All these changes make the muscle shorter and less elastic. As the muscle eventually heals, scar tissue binds muscles and tendons together, making them even less flexible. As a result, greater pressures are placed on the inelastic tendons. This strain to tendons results in most of the physical causes of RSI, including tendon inflammation, friction, and pressure on nearby nerves and blood vessels.

Ironically, many of the processes that lead to debilitating RSI are the body's protective responses to injury or strain. Inflammation following an injury actually speeds recovery by sending lots of blood to the area. White blood cells clear out damaged tissues in the area, and the increased blood flow takes waste products away. The swelling associated with inflammation stiffens the body part to keep the person from injuring it further, and muscle tension around the area automatically makes it stiffer still. The tightness from inflammation can lead to painful pressure on the nerves. This is the body's way of saying, "Lay off before you hurt yourself more."[3] The connective tissue that holds the muscles together also becomes denser, tighter, and stickier, protecting the injured part like a cast.

The trouble with RSI is that people may not listen to these bodily responses, or they choose not to because they do not want to lose their job or do not want to appear weak.[4] Injury leads to further injury as long as the repetitive motions continue.

RSI is the cumulative effect of many microscopic traumas that occur over time.

RSI includes several related disorders affecting tendons, tendon sheaths, muscles, and nerves. The disorders have complicated names like cervical radiculopathy, thoracic outlet syndrome, distal ulnar neuropathy, and cubital tunnel syndrome. But all of them share the same origin in repetitive strain. They can be broken down, for simplicity, into tendon disorders, nerve disorders, and neurovascular disorders, which affect both nerves and blood vessels.

## Tendon Disorders

Unlike muscles, the tendons that connect muscles to bone do not contract or stretch. Normally they transfer the action of muscles into the motion of bones faithfully and without complaining. But if they are subjected to repetitive motions at the same time as other risk factors, including injury and stiffness of muscles, they will, in turn, be injured. Tiny tears and adhesions will develop, or inflammation will occur from increased friction, called tendinitis. Because tendons have very little blood supply, tendinitis takes a long time to heal. Tendons often heal poorly, with gobs of scar tissue binding them together, making them thick and bumpy. Injured tendons can be very painful, and the tendons are likely to tear again.

Examples of tendinitis are many, and it seems there is not a tendon in the body that is not exposed to repetitive motion by some activity. Extensor tendinitis is inflammation of the tendon in the back of the wrist that straightens the fingers. It is often found in computer users who rest their hands on the desk. This position requires the tendon and the extensor muscle on the top of the forearm to do all the work of moving the fingers over the keyboard. All that fancy finger work is better served by the stronger muscles of the arm and shoulder than by the tiny extensor muscle, which is about the thickness of a pencil. Extensor tendinitis is also common among musicians who play stringed instruments. It results from pressing on the strings too hard with their left hands. Flexor tendinitis, on the other hand, affects the tendons that bend the fingers. It is found among "clackers," people who hit the keyboard with too much force, or among people who grip the mouse too tightly.

Tennis elbow, also known as lateral epicondylitis, is another example of tendinitis. The extensor muscle on top of the forearm attaches to a tendon at a tiny spot on the outside of the elbow. This point of attachment is vulnerable to injury if repeated motions involve lifting heavy objects, scrubbing floors, pouring lots of coffee, or, of course, playing tennis. The tendon tears in a V shape, which is very hard to heal and easy to reinjure. Golfer's elbow, or medial epicondylitis, is the opposite of tennis elbow. It involves the tendon that attaches the flexor muscle in the forearm to the inside of the elbow. Tendinitis here results from repeated forceful rotation accompanied by bending the wrist, as in scrubbing pots, lifting weights, or swinging a golf club. Tendinitis of the elbow is on the rise among computer users with aggressive tendencies in using the mouse.

Where tendons pass through tight spots or around corners, as in the wrist and fingers, they are covered by a sheath called a synovium. Normally, the tendons slide easily back and forth within this sheath, or tunnel, much like a bicycle brake cable slides through its housing. The tendons are lubricated by synovial fluid. For example, to move a finger from fully flexed to fully extended some tendons may slide up to two inches.

Excessive tension caused by the many possible risk factors, combined with repetitions of 1,500 to 2,000 per hour, are more

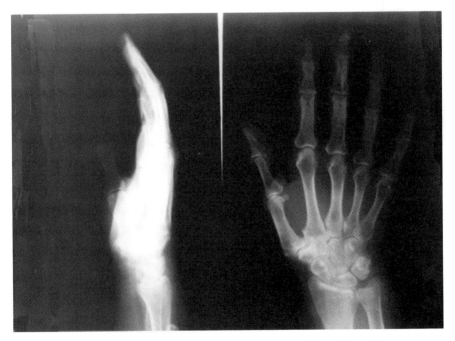

The muscles that move the hand are connected to its bones by tendons.

than the tendon and sheath can endure.[5] The tendon becomes rough and irritated, and the sheath responds by swelling and producing excess fluid, a disorder called tenosynovitis.

Tenosynovitis can be a debilitating and painful problem in its own right. The swelling will go down, and the synovium can heal, but it may be tighter than before, creating the potential for further injury. The most common example of this occurs in a tendon at the base of the thumb near the wrist. This painful problem is called deQuervain's disease, and it is found among people who frequently do a wringing motion with their hands or who hold their thumbs up when they type. It can also occur in people who have a new baby and lift the precious bundle with their thumbs extended.

The extreme case of tenosynovitis goes by the impressive name *stenosing tenosynovitis crepitans*, also known as trigger finger. In the case of trigger finger, the sheath becomes so hardened and swollen that the tendon becomes stuck. The affected finger is frozen in a bent position or moves with jerky motions.

## Nerve Disorders

Nerve damage can be caused by repeated pressure on nerves from external sharp edges or hard surfaces. For example, telephone operator's elbow is a numbness in the little finger and arm that results from resting one's arm on the edge of the table, and surfer's knee comes from kneeling on a hard surfboard. But nerve disorders are also associated with swollen tendons and synovial sheaths, resulting in crowding. In tight places the swollen tissues can put pressure on nerves, producing pain, numbness, and other symptoms. These are the tunnel syndromes, so called because they occur in areas where nerves, tendons, and other tissues are all trying to squeeze through narrow spaces. When there is inflammation in the area, the pressure on the nerves results in pain, weakness, and numbness. Unlike tendinitis, the pain does not necessarily get better with rest.

Unfortunately, the long course of the nerves to the hand provides many locations for the nerves to be compressed by a variety of actions. Carpal tunnel syndrome (CTS) is the most commonly known disorder of this type, and it is often equated with RSI; however, there are many other tunnel syndromes. CTS occurs when the median nerve that runs down the underside of the wrist is compressed by neighboring tissues. Nine tendons squeeze together with this nerve through the carpal tunnel, a tiny space one inch long and bound by the wrist bones and the tough ligament that goes across the base of the hand. It is bumper-to-bumper traffic in the carpal tunnel, and when the lining of the tunnel swells there is nowhere to go but crashing into the median nerve.

People may contract CTS from activities that require repetitive up-and-down movements of the wrist, such as using hand tools, weight training, playing racquetball, or from typing on a computer with tipped-up wrists. CTS sufferers often experience weakness, pain, burning, tingling, numbness, and aching in their hands. It is often so severe at night that it wakes them up. CTS can be associated with other medical conditions that result in fluid retention, making the carpal tunnel even tighter. These conditions include rheumatoid arthritis, leukemia, thyroid disorders, and diabetes. Women who are pregnant, in menopause, or taking oral contraceptives are more susceptible because hormonal changes associated with these conditions also cause fluid retention. This may be partly why CTS is three times as common in women.[6]

Other tunnel syndromes are not as common as CTS, but they can be equally as debilitating. Ulnar tunnel syndrome occurs when the ulnar nerve is compressed as it runs through a shallow groove, right next to the carpal tunnel, on its way to the pinkie finger. This can be caused by frequent flexing of the wrist back and inward or by compression on external surfaces. German doctors found it in soldiers during World War II who had to ride bicycles over great distances; they gave it the imposing name *Radfahrerlähung*.[7] Cubital tunnel syndrome afflicts the ulnar nerve as it passes through a tight spot at the elbow. It is experienced by people who work with their elbows bent for long periods, such as truck drivers, phone operators, and cellists. Cubital tunnel syndrome results in pain, tingling, and weakness in the hand and forearm.

There are many other tunnel syndromes, including radial tunnel syndrome, which affects the radial nerve in the forearm, and tarsal tunnel syndrome, which affects the nerve running through the ankle to the feet. They share the common problem of nerve compression caused either by external surfaces or by inflammation of neighboring tissues from overuse.

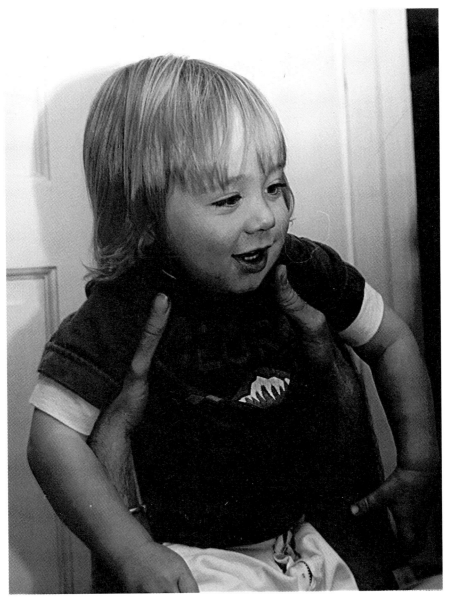

Sometimes the first hint of RSI comes during motions unrelated to the source of injury, like lifting a baby.

## Neurovascular Disorders

RSI can interfere with circulation as well as the nervous system, as in the case of neurovascular disorders. The most outstanding of these is thoracic outlet syndrome (TOS). TOS is experienced by many musicians and other people who must hold their arms extended for long periods, such as double bassists, guitarists, and harpists. It especially affects those with poor posture. The thoracic outlet is the internal region where the neck, chest, and one shoulder meet. Deep within that area, a bundle of nerves and blood vessels passes through other tissues on their way to the arm. The bundle is susceptible to compression at several sites, mostly by muscles in the neck. Compression of these nerves and arteries causes pain in the entire area and numbness and weakness in the fingers and hand.

Another neurovascular RSI is called Raynaud's phenomenon or, most descriptive and creepy, white finger. White finger results from a loss of circulation to the finger, most often triggered by cold external conditions. But it can also occur when the arteries leading to the fingers are forced shut

## Expensive Injuries

United States businesses spend 2 billion dollars every year on furniture and workstation accessories designed to prevent RSIs.

by forceful gripping of an object, overuse of a vibrating tool, or riding a motorcycle. People may feel numbness or loss of control of their fingers, as well as notice the eerie paleness that earns this disorder its name.

## The Many Faces of RSI

The various forms of RSI can range from a minor inconvenience to a life-shattering debility. For Jane, it meant quitting her job at the cafeteria and enduring years of discomfort. She experienced flare-ups during her pregnancy, even though she was not working. It hurt to rake leaves or mow the lawn. Now she works at a bank and only notices occasional twinges when she gets a little too aggressive with the computer mouse. Like many other people who have suffered from RSI, it changed her life forever.[8]

Every case of RSI is different because people's bodies and circumstances are different. Jane might have never experienced RSI as a computer user if she had not also been a cafeteria worker. Although this chapter has simplified the physical changes and symptoms associated with RSI for the sake of brevity, RSI is not a simple problem. Each person is affected by the disease differently and contributes to its development with his or her own individual habits and activities. The first step in stemming the tide of RSI is recognizing risk factors— those activities or circumstances that are risky.

# 4

# Repetition as a Way of Life

Leon Fleisher has been regarded as one of the finest
American pianists of his generation. He has been playing
piano since as long as he can remember. He made his
Carnegie Hall debut at age sixteen and became an instant
celebrity when he won a prestigious competition at the age of
twenty-four. After that, he performed all over the world to
grateful audiences. But fame had its cost, and he spent long
hours at the piano, practicing and rehearsing. "I wanted to
sustain this career," he says, "and that's when I started
overworking."[1]

Leon's brilliant career was at its peak when he noticed a
problem: the little finger on his right hand felt weak. He tried
practicing harder and longer, reaching for those high notes
with a vengeance, but the finger did not respond. In fact, it
curled under as if it were defending itself. As if that were not

bad enough, the fourth finger soon followed. Over the next ten months, to the musician's horror, the rest of his right hand curled up like a withered leaf, potentially taking his career with it. "I was in the deepest despair," he says. "There's no question but that suicide entered my mind."[2]

Thirty years ago, when Leon first suffered from RSI, there was not even a name for his ailment. Doctors had little idea how to correct his problem, and he has spent the latter half of his life trying to deal with it physically and emotionally. These days more and more doctors have a better idea of how to recognize and treat RSI. They realize that certain risk factors

Musicians have been subject to RSIs for centuries because of the many hours of rigorous practice required.

make some people more likely to contract RSI than others, and they can identify the symptoms and distinguish them from other problems. Finally, they have a firm understanding of the various physical causes that underlie RSI.

## Risk Factors: How RSI Begins

When someone skis into a tree and breaks his arm, there is little doubt of what caused the injury. But RSI is usually caused by multiple risk factors that overlap and intertwine, so it is not as simple to identify the source of the injury. First among risk factors is repetitive motions, whether they come from playing a piano like Leon Fleisher, hammering nails, or scrubbing pots. It is repetitive motion that provokes the cumulative trauma of muscles and tendons and the symptoms identified as RSI. But repetition is not enough, or else RSI would be experienced by every pianist, carpenter, and pot scrubber. There is a suite of other risk factors—including genetic factors or other physical predispositions, posture and positioning, conditioning, and psychological factors such as stress—any of which can make repetition a dangerous thing. Each risk factor can contribute to muscle strain by working against the muscles, making them rigid and fatigued. The more risk factors that are combined, the more likely that RSI is on the horizon.

## Genetic Risk Factors and Habits

Variety is the spice of life! Everyone is delightfully different, but the downside of these differences is that some people may be more likely to suffer from RSI because of their genetic heritage, physical build, or habits. For instance, women are more likely than men to have RSI, partly because they generally have slighter builds. Women also make up the majority of computer operators, telephone operators, and other workers with similar hand-intensive tasks. Women are also more likely to suffer from RSI if they are pregnant or using oral contraceptives because of the fluid retention associated with these conditions.

Men who have slighter builds have the same predisposition for RSI that women do. Ironically, obesity is also a risk factor. Overweight people have to exert more pressure to hold their arms up in any given position, such as over a keyboard, and may also have to assume contorted positions to reach tools around their own bulk. Double-jointedness is also a liability because it can put extra stress on muscles and tendons. The average age of RSI sufferers is thirty-nine, but it is bound to go down as more and more young people join the computer age with all its potential bad habits.[3]

## Health-Related Risk Factors

Many health risks can contribute to the onset of RSI, including smoking, alcoholism, or poor eating or sleeping habits. Each of these adds stress to anyone's physical strength and can make her more easily injured. Certain diseases are also risk factors, such as rheumatoid arthritis, hypertension, diabetes, thyroid problems, or kidney disease. All these problems change the fluid balance and chemistry of the blood, compressing tissues and, in turn, making fatigue and injury more likely. Traumatic accidents such as skiing into a tree can complicate or increase the risk of RSI, even if the injury occurred years ago. Anything that weakens or tightens muscles, making their work more difficult, can be a factor.

## Recreational Activities as Risk Factors

If RSI were encountered only on the job, it could be avoided by never going to work—not a feasible alternative for most people. But even activities that people find relaxing can be potential risk factors for RSI. Many athletic or recreational activities, such as fishing, bowling, tennis, or golf, require repetitive motions that can contribute to the injury. Something as innocent as knitting, sewing, or playing the guitar can also be a strain, especially if there are other risks involved, such as a lack of rest or improper body positioning or posture.

This is not to say that these enjoyable activities should be avoided. In many cases they may be helpful in conditioning, stretching, or reducing the stress in muscles and tendons injured at work. But recreational activities must be approached with the same attention to proper technique and adequate breaks as the most grueling assembly-line job. There are times when it is difficult to distinguish which risks are most responsible for a person's RSI. For example, a person may be an overworked computer operator on the weekdays and an avid knitter on weekends and evenings. In most cases it is probably a combination of work-related and nonwork-related activities that contributes to the RSI.

## Posture and Positioning

Next to repetitive motions, perhaps the most important risk factor is the posture and positioning with which those motions are made. Your body is supremely designed for certain activities, and unfortunately, hanging plasterboard, packing chicken legs, and typing memos for hours on end are not among them. People who stand or walk with good posture do what the body does best: They align all their bones and muscles

Old manual typewriters required the strength of your whole arm to operate, enforcing proper positioning.

so that they are perfectly supported against gravity. Gravity never takes a break. Whenever a body part is out of line, such as when slouching over a computer keyboard or reaching for a chicken leg on an assembly line, gravity pulls on that part. The constant resistance to this pull can lead to strain and potential injury.

There is more to fighting gravity than meets the eye. Your body performs two types of actions: dynamic and static. Hitting a nail with a hammer is dynamic action. The muscles in the arm tense and relax in sequence, which helps pump blood into and out of the muscles. When each muscle relaxes, blood flows in, providing vital nutrients and oxygen. When the muscle tenses, it squeezes blood out, taking with it carbon dioxide and other waste products produced by the muscles. Repetitive dynamic action can eventually lead to fatigue and strain, but the pumping action of muscles helps to resist it.

Resisting gravity, on the other hand, requires static action. Slouching over an assembly-line conveyor belt is static action. The lower back muscles are tensed to hold a position, continually forcing blood out of the muscles. No pumping takes place, so the muscles are deprived of oxygen and nutrients and are swamped with their own waste products. If the muscles are working at anything more than 15 percent of their maximum strength, then the blood supply that creeps in cannot meet the demands of the muscle. The buildup of wastes and the starvation for nutrients leads to the feeling of fatigue. If this imbalance persists, the muscles become inflamed, or sore and swollen.[4]

Bad posture is a strain on your muscles, whether you are sitting or standing. Your back is designed to support your shoulders and head in a balanced way. If it is out of balance, then your muscles are constantly working against gravity. Bad postural habits begin with childhood and are reinforced through development by psychological factors such as self-consciousness or shyness. By the time one is an adult, bad posture feels normal, and the imbalanced use of back muscles is very hard to correct. Holding one's body straight and stiff to try to correct one's posture is no better and can lead to tension and strain in the muscles as well. Whether working at a computer or playing golf, bad posture can contribute to the tension of other related muscles and lead to RSI.

Holding other parts of the body incorrectly during repetitive motions is another risk factor. As with posture, your arms are designed to work in a balanced way. They are strongest at the midpoint of normal motion, called neutral position—not too far contracted or extended. You are more likely to strain your shoulder if you repeatedly lift your arms above shoulder level or bend your arm behind your body, as a cashier does when pushing groceries along, because these motions are at the limits of your muscles' motion. Likewise, elbow movements that rotate the joint inward and outward, as in tennis, will strain the muscles that are attached there. Your wrist is sensitive to being pushed too far back or forward, as well as to twisting left or right. Your fingers can be strained by too much bending or grasping. All these strained positions, when combined with repetitive motions, can potentially lead to RSI. Angler's elbow,

Many of the habits that can contribute to RSI, such as poor posture, begin at an early age.

for instance, is caused by fishing with a hard grip on the fishing rod or by twisting the wrist while casting.

A position commonly found among computer users is with the wrist resting on the table and the hands arched up to reach the keys. Bending the wrist up like this is called dorsiflexion, and it severely stretches the muscles on the front of the wrist, making them and their tendons vulnerable to RSI. Because the arm is resting on the table, the fingers have to strain to reach the keys, rather than being moved around more easily by the stronger arm muscles. Many typists also bend their wrists to the outside so that their fingers line up with the keys better, a position called ulnar deviation because the wrists are bent toward the ulnar bone, which runs along the outside of the forearm. Again, this strains muscles and tendons in the forearm, making them vulnerable.

Young people are spending more and more time in front of computers and are therefore very susceptible to RSI if poor positioning habits are not corrected. Other habits to avoid are striking the keys too hard, resting elbows on chair arms, and contorting the fingers while typing. Even gripping the mouse too tightly and clicking it too hard, like Clara did, can lead to

# Professional Postures[5]

Many professions share motions or postures that can lead to the same injury, such as

- computer operators, secretaries, and pianists (sitting still, rapid finger movements, wrists cocked, elbows bent)
- meat processors, carpet layers, welders (grasping, cutting, and guiding with arms elevated)
- carpenters, taxi drivers, domestic workers (grasping, with wrist flexed and elbow bent)
- trash haulers, stone masons, warehouse workers (repetitive heavy lifting with tight gripping)
- assemblers, surgeons, needleworkers, architects (fine, precise finger and thumb movements while looking down with head forward)

muscle fatigue and RSI. Mouse use accounts for two thirds of computer time on average, and many people place their mouse pad too far away to use without straining. The trouble with all these position factors are that bad habits are hard to change, so starting out with good habits when you are young puts you at an advantage.

# Deconditioning

Despite recent public interest in being fit, many Americans are still out of shape, especially when it comes to their hands. When muscles are out of shape, or deconditioned, they become tight and rigid, reducing the amount of blood circulating through them. When they are then used beyond their limits, they quickly become stiff from the lack of nutrients and the buildup of toxic wastes. There is a misconception that computer work, as well as many of the other light manual activities that can lead to RSI, is easy work. In fact, it takes incredible conditioning to sit at a desk for eight hours or more and type thousands of words, or to stand and assemble appliances for hours on end, every day. Even the most able-bodied athletes do not achieve that kind of endurance.

Deconditioning can be very complicated. Many repetitive motions exercise certain muscles at the expense of others, so the muscles become unequal in strength and cannot work in concert. This can add to the muscle strain from the repetitive motions. A carefully balanced conditioning regimen is required to bring the muscles back into equilibrium. Tendons also stop growing by the time a person reaches adulthood. If someone increases the strength of his muscles later in life, he is actually more likely to injure his tendons because he could put more pressure on them than they were designed for. For many RSI-risk tasks, all that is required for proper conditioning is some variety: time to warm up muscles and recovery time in the form of breaks or other tasks that require different motions. More details on conditioning can be found in Chapter 8.

## Stress and Psychological Risk Factors

Many RSI-sufferers often overlook stress as a risk factor. There are a lot of stresses in one's life, and many of them can be positive, like getting married, getting a promotion at work, or buying a house. But some workplaces feature negative stressors that can impact a worker's well-being. Smoky, noisy, cramped, or badly lit working conditions are just the beginning. Some jobs come with long hours and fast-paced and high-pressure atmospheres. Some jobs feature a monitoring system that keeps track of workers' productivity, driving them to work harder and worry about their job security. Although stressful working conditions are primarily psychological, stress results in physical reactions. The physiological response to stress includes changes in breathing, heart rate, posture, and muscle balance, all of which can contribute to RSI.

Even attitude can be a risk factor. Many people ignore the first twinges of pain or discomfort from RSI because of a concern about their image. Some people feel driven to do their work and disregard the symptoms as just a part of the job. Shy people are at risk because they may be less likely to complain to their superiors and let their needs be known. A worker's emotional state can also make him more likely to have RSI. If he is anxious and depressed about things outside of work, it can influence his posture and stress level at work.

The risk factors that contribute to RSI include genetic predisposition, health factors, posture and positioning, deconditioning, and stress. Each of these works in its own way to make the muscles work harder and become more rigid, more fatigued, and more strained. When the muscles are compromised like this, they also make the tendons do more than their share of the work. Far too often the result is injury to the tendons and the debilitating symptoms of RSI.

# 5

# Finding the Pain

To the concert pianist Leon Fleisher, who was introduced in Chapter 4, RSI meant he could no longer express himself as he always had. Although he rallied to continue performing, specializing in pieces written for only one hand, he contented himself mostly with teaching others to play. The turning point for Fleisher came when someone accurately identified the cause of his disability. He had seen every kind of doctor and tried all kinds of therapy, from drugs to hypnosis. Then finally, after thirty years of frustration with his withered right hand, he found someone who could help him. This person identified his predicament as a repetitive strain injury and treated it with a form of deep tissue massage called Rolfing. The manipulation of the connective tissue in his hand, wrist, and arm allowed his hand to get softer and more supple. By 1995, he was playing two-handed again, and less than a year later he was performing at Carnegie Hall.[1]

The solution to Leon Fleisher's symptoms would not necessarily benefit a meat packer, a carpenter, a secretary, or even another pianist. Treating his symptoms took a deep understanding of his lifestyle and movements, as well as of the strengths and weaknesses of muscles and tendons and the various forms of RSI. The complexity of RSI requires an intimate knowledge of all these factors.

The first step in treating RSI, as in any disease, is diagnosis. There is no point in treating someone with radial tunnel syndrome for tennis elbow, because the treatments may be very different. Some doctors assume that RSI symptoms are caused by carpal tunnel syndrome and stop there, despite the fact that CTS makes up a small percentage of RSIs.[2] The most complete picture of the patient's RSI will include a history of the patient's experience, an analysis of her workstation and habits, a physical exam, and laboratory tests.

## Getting to Know the RSI Patient

The patient's history is a window to the source of his RSI. First of all, he is the only one who can identify exactly where and when symptoms occur, and what activities they are related to. Common activities of daily living, or ADLs, are useful in monitoring the severity and location of an injury. How the injury feels when one is brushing teeth, brushing hair, chopping vegetables, opening doors, turning faucets, or opening jars is all valuable information and should be cataloged by the patient or doctor. Knowing about the workstation design and work habits or other activities that may have contributed to the injury is also useful to an insightful doctor. Ideally, the doctor would actually watch the patient perform these activities because there are many habits that the patient may not be aware of. For instance, the patient may not know that he types with his pinkies in the air or drives with clenched knuckles—habits that could be contributing to his RSI.

## The Physical Exam

The physical exam of an RSI patient involves many levels. First, the doctor will merely inspect the afflicted part to look for visible swellings or other symptoms. Then, she will perform a series of movement tests to assess the possible range of motion and to narrow down the source of the symptoms. The movements tested are either passive, active, or resisted and are intended to re-create the pain or other symptoms experienced by the patient. A combination of all types of movements is useful in diagnosing RSI and other types of injuries.

Active movements (when the patient moves his own body parts) can help pinpoint which movements are painful, but they can be misleading about the source of the symptom. Passive movements (when the doctor moves the patient's hand or arm unassisted by the patient) are especially painful when the injury is to ligaments or joints. Resisted movement (when

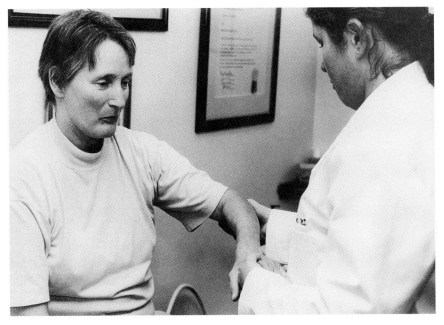

Patients who seek help for the first signs of RSI have the greatest chance of full recovery.

the patient pushes against equal pressure by the doctor) is most useful in isolating which muscle-tendon unit is involved.

Many of these motions have particular names. Phalen's test for CTS involves pushing the patient's wrist down, or flexing it, as far as it will go. Wormser's test is the opposite, pulling the wrist back as far as it will go. Although both these motions are usually painless to an uninjured patient, they can be excruciating to someone with CTS and are therefore useful in its diagnosis. Finkelstein's sign is a test for deQuervain's disease, the tenosynovitis at the base of the thumb. The doctor will ask the patient to make a fist with his thumb curled in the middle, then bend his wrist down toward the pinkie and ask him if it hurts. Again, it sounds as if it probably would, but this test is only painful to someone with deQuervain's.

Other tests may not involve movement but light touching, tapping, or pressure to the arm or hand. The Semmes-Weinstein monofilament test requires a piece of monofilament, also known as fishing line, to test the sensitivity to light touch. The tapping of fingers can test for the presence of tingling feelings. Tinel's sign for CTS is a tapping on the tough ligament overlying the carpal tunnel. Bilic's pressure test involves pressing the nerve itself. The most extreme of these manipulations

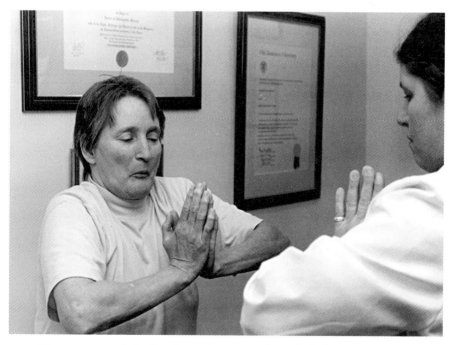

There are several simple diagnostic tests, such as Phalen's maneuver, that help narrow the diagnosis.

is a temporary tourniquet, a tight band around the arm that cuts off circulation. Nerves that are compressed by injury are very sensitive to this diagnostic method.

## Diagnostic Tools

After the patient's history is taken and the physical exam is completed, further tests may be in order to narrow the diagnosis or to verify a final diagnosis. These tests include X rays, electrodiagnostic tests, angiograms, magnetic resonance imaging (MRI), and computed tomography (CT).

X rays are not the most useful diagnostic tool for RSI, but they are a simple measure for eliminating many things that are easily confused with it. X rays can only show bones, so if the culprit is injured muscles, swollen tendons, compressed nerves, or scar tissue, the X rays will not detect them unless a tendon tears from a bone and takes a tiny piece of bone with it.

Electrodiagnostic testing takes two forms. In nerve conduction velocity (NCV) tests, electrodes are attached to two parts of the hand, and the adjacent nerves are activated by a stimulation bar. It is a race to see which nerve conducts the electrical impulse faster, a test commonly used for diagnosing CTS. By measuring the speed of the electrical impulse passing through the median nerve, which is compressed by CTS, and the neighboring ulnar nerve, a comparison is possible. If the current through the median nerve is prolonged more than four milliseconds, it loses the race, and that is evidence for compression, or CTS.[3]

The other form of electrodiagnosis records the electrical conduction of normal muscle activity. The electromyogram (EMG) test involves probing different muscles with a stimulation needle and asking the patient to move the part against resistance. The EMG machine detects damage to the nerves that stimulate muscles, which can be even more serious than damage to sensory nerves, because this leads to muscle atrophy.

Doctors resort to tests called angiograms when the constriction of a blood vessel is suspected. This test is more invasive and unpleasant because a dye is injected into the circulatory system. The dye can then be seen with an X ray, and any compression of the blood vessels can be detected.

Magnetic resonance imaging and computed tomography are two high-tech forms of scans that are increasingly common despite their high cost. They both make it possible to see detailed images of internal anatomy. CT is particularly good at showing internal bony anatomy, and MRI can clearly show

# Illness or Injury?

The U.S. Bureau of Labor Statistics keeps track of repetitive strain injuries in the workplace. Since 1972, RSI has been classified as an illness, not an injury, because it is not the result of a sudden traumatic event. But the new standards put in place by the Occupational Safety and Health Administration include removing RSI from the illness category and requiring the reporting of all cases of RSI.[4]

tears and inflammation of tendons and other soft tissue. Their value in diagnosing RSI is obvious, especially in anatomical areas that involve many layers of muscles and other soft tissues, such as the shoulder.

If the diagnosis shows that the patient's RSI is not too severe, then there is a good chance the patient will be almost back to normal someday. But muscles, tendons, and nerves can take months to heal, and consistent effort on the part of the patient is necessary for them to heal correctly. They are very fragile while they are healing and can easily be reinjured, making the healing process more difficult and incomplete in the end. The injury will always be a weak spot, but if the RSI sufferer is patient with his body and follows his treatment regimen closely, then RSI will be a thing of his past.

# Healing the Strain

**F**or many people with RSI, the first step toward starting to heal has to be stopping the pain caused by inflammation. Some of them have ignored their symptoms for so long that it has become debilitating, and others have been struck with severe symptoms without warning. The most important part of pain management is often hardest: stop the offending activity. Do not play tennis, play guitar, or answer e-mail. Do not go to work if that is the source of the injury, or find activities at work that use different motions. If you must continue the activity, do so at a modified pace and learn to stop *before* the pain begins. Working in spite of pain will just compound the injury. Ice on the sore part can reduce the inflammation and swelling that causes pain. Heat, on the other hand, can help soothe and relax tense muscles. Gently massaging and stretching the area may also ease pain.

Warmth not only helps soothe muscles, but also brings circulation to the area and speeds the healing process by supplying oxygen and taking away debris, toxins, and other waste products that build up during inflammation. The heat may be in the form of an electric heating pad, a hot-water bottle, a hot bath, or, for deeper penetrating heat, ultrasound therapy. Ultrasound involves the projection of very high-frequency sound waves through the soft tissues. The sound waves travel to the bone and return through the tissues again. They vibrate the molecules in these tissues, like strings on a guitar, and warm them from the inside. This therapy is used with caution on patients with nerve compression, but it can be very helpful to patients with RSIs affecting their muscles and tendons.[1]

RSI sufferers may have to modify other parts of their lives to help manage their pain, including the activities of daily living mentioned before. An occupational therapist can help identify painful ADLs and suggest how to change them. These changes may include having shorter hair that requires less brushing, going for smaller shopping trips, using sharper knives, using mechanical jar openers, or using the shoulder to open doors. These suggestions may appear to be common sense, but they can be extremely helpful to someone overwhelmed with pain. He or she may even have to negotiate with family or friends for more help with chores and other ADLs. In addition to managing the pain, adapting ADLs can help speed the healing process and prevent reinjury.

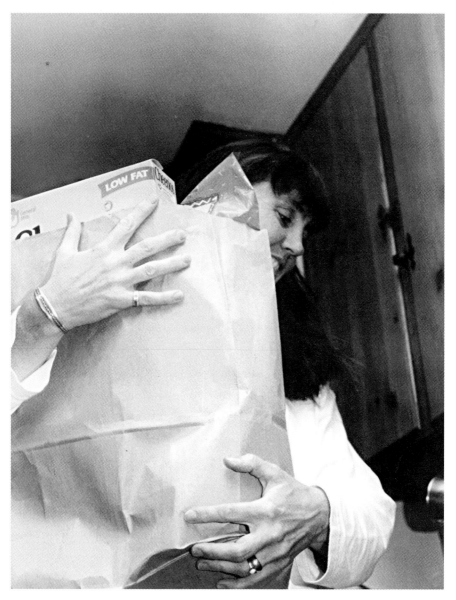

Many of the activities of daily living that contribute to a patient's RSI may have to be modified or supplemented with the help of friends or family.

# Drug Therapy

Many doctors encourage the use of drug therapy for RSI patients to relieve the pain while healing takes place. The drugs used are either anti-inflammatories, analgesics, or muscle relaxants. Anti-inflammatory drugs, such as ibuprofen, are good when there is a minor injury, but in serious cases they bring only temporary relief. Because they fight inflammation, they also interfere with the removal of waste products, which is one of the roles of inflammation and an important part of the healing process. They can have several other side effects, including ulcers, stomach cramps, nausea, chills, fluid retention, and liver damage over the long term.[2]

Analgesics numb the pain while the patient gets better, and for some patients, that is an incredible relief. These drugs, including codeine and Demerol (meperidine), are so effective that they can often give the patient a false sense of security. They may make it comfortable to continue overusing the body part and to perform activities that are harmful to the healing process. Muscle relaxants such as Valium (diazepam) and Robaxin (methocarbamol) also provide temporary relief from pain, especially when stress or muscle tension is involved. Once again, drug therapy can be a valuable boost in the healing process, as well as in the peace of mind of the patient.

# Splinting

Another part of RSI treatment often involves immobilization or restricted motion of the affected part through splinting.

Resting the injured part is critical to its healing process and can temporarily alleviate symptoms. However, splinting is a more controversial measure. Immobilization leads to weakening of muscles, range-of-motion loss, and sloppy scar tissue growth. Ironically, these conditions are many of the risk factors that can lead to RSI in the first place.[3] Patients who use splints are recommended to take the splint off regularly to allow some movement and gentle massaging. Splinting can also contribute to the overuse of other muscles and may lead to injuries elsewhere. This measure is only currently recommended in combination with other treatments, especially in cases where nerve compression is at risk, such as in CTS.

## Injections

Another common treatment for RSI is the injection of hydrocortisone, a steroid hormone derivative, to stop the inflammation. It avoids many of the side effects of other drugs and allows the active agent to be applied directly to the site of injury. Inflammation is stopped in its tracks, preventing the development of unwanted scar tissue. It can produce apparently miraculous results, making an RSI patient previously crippled by pain symptom-free in a matter of days.[4] It can be overdone, however, as repetitive injections can actually damage the tendons and bones of the joint.[5] Cortisone can alternatively be applied as a cream or spray to the affected area and may be combined with ultrasound therapy for effective results.

Another RSI therapy involves the injection of proliferants. These drugs promote the production of new tissue. Previously it was thought that tendons could not form new cells once they were fully grown. But proliferants can induce the cells of tendons to reproduce, speeding the process of recovery from tendinitis. This relatively new treatment has great potential for healing RSIs.

## Surgery

Surgery may be used as a last resort if RSI involves the chronic compression of nerves, as in the case of CTS. If other therapies are not effective in stopping CTS symptoms within six

# RSI Acronyms

The names of repetitive strain injuries and their diagnostic tests and treatments are often shortened into acronyms. Here is a list of the acronyms used in this book:

CT—computed tomography
CTS—carpal tunnel syndrome
EMG—electromyography
MRI—magnetic resonance imaging
NCV—nerve conduction velocity
RSI—repetitive strain injury
TENS—transcutaneous electrical nerve stimulation
TOS—thoracic outlet syndrome

months, surgery is recommended. Continuing conservative measures any longer than that reduces the chance of good results from the surgery. Surgery for CTS involves freeing the pinched nerve by cutting through the tough ligament that makes up the roof of the carpal tunnel. This can now be performed through endoscopic surgery, which involves inserting a small fiber-optic tube like a periscope into the wrist through a tiny incision. The patient usually has immediate relief from symptoms and is released from the hospital the same day. There is a 97 percent success rate with this procedure if the patient has had symptoms for less than six months.[6]

Surgery may be performed for other nerve compression cases or to free the tendon at the base of the thumb in deQuervain's disease. But these are less common and are usually used as a last resort. Even in the case of CTS sufferers, surgery is only a temporary solution if there is no modification of the work environment, habits, or lifestyle.[7] The repetition has to stop.

## Rehabilitation

Despite making the best efforts to rest, massage the area, and use drug therapy, injections, and even surgery, in the end the RSI patient is still responsible for the healing. As soon as the injured part can be moved without pain, the patient should begin doing exercises as prescribed by a physical therapist. If she does not, she could lose 20 percent of her muscle power within two weeks. Muscles begin to atrophy, or break down and become weak. Tendons can lose part of their mineral content and become more fragile, making them more vulnerable to reinjury. Scar tissue develops and adheres to other tissues, limiting movement. Anyone who has ever had a serious injury would recognize the stiffness associated with this scar tissue formation. Ironically, movement was responsible for the injury and movement is necessary to promote positive and flexible healing. This is the process of rehabilitation.

Rehabilitation may be boring, but there is no way around it. It involves repetition of simple exercises involving five to ten repetitions of a movement, with about thirty seconds of rest before the next movement. Ice may be applied during the exercises to reduce inflammation so that movements can be performed with more flexibility and less pain. The number of exercises or repetitions prescribed by the physical therapist increases very gradually as healing progresses. The regimen requires incredible patience. It is not appropriate to jump ahead to more difficult movements, including the repetitive movements that caused the injury. Slow and steady movements are necessary to get the injured part up to speed and integrated with the rest of the body before the patient can get on with his life.

## Reconditioning

The next steps in recovery are reconditioning and occupational therapy. Reconditioning strengthens the muscles so that further injury is less likely and occupational therapy corrects harmful postures or habits at work. The RSI sufferer

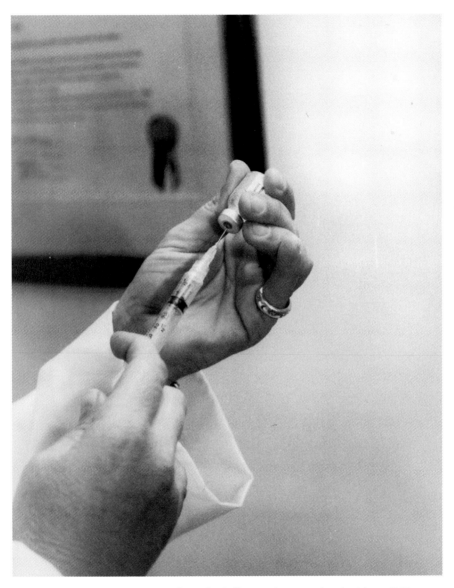

Cortisone injections can reduce the inflammation associated with an RSI and speed healing in some cases.

still has to be patient at this point and not overdo it, or she will reinjure herself. She has to gradually do more strenuous exercises, such as swimming or stretching, without jumping ahead to racquetball. She may be asked to work out regularly on an upper body exerciser (UBE), which is like a bicycle for the arms. Months of tedious reconditioning may be more than a patient can stand, but it is the only way to heal completely. The key is to condition muscles in a balanced way, as described in Chapter 4, so that some muscles are not leaving others to do the work.

## Occupational Therapy

Occupational therapy allows RSI patients to reassess how they do their work. They learn how to protect their muscles, how to position themselves correctly, and how to pace themselves to avoid injury. An occupational therapist can suggest additional stretching and strengthening exercises that are specific to the injury and the repetitive motions required. He can watch someone at work and recommend changes in the workstation or work habits that will allow the patient to work without becoming injured again. Physical therapists who specialize in sports injuries can observe the patient's tennis technique or golf swing and recommend positive changes.

Video analysis is a powerful tool for helping RSI sufferers overcome their dangerous postures and habits at work or play. Video feedback involves taping someone performing his usual activities at several angles, whether it is working at the computer, playing a cello, or swinging a tennis racquet. Then the patient can observe his own mistakes in position or technique, many of which he is probably not aware of. This is much more convincing than simply being told he has bad habits. Even more powerful is the process of biofeedback for reducing unconscious and invisible muscle tension. Electrodes are used to detect the force being applied by specific muscles—for instance, those in a cellist's hand—and a computer reads out the results while the subject performs the activity.

## Alternative Therapies

Several practices that exist at the fringes of normal medicine are valuable tools for dealing with RSI. These alternative therapies may not be condoned by every physician, but most will agree to their use under a doctor's guidance. Perhaps the most widely accepted of these practices is massage. Massage helps keep muscles supple and stretched during the healing process. Muscle tension is a normal reaction to any trauma, preventing the circulation of blood with its oxygen and nutrients. Massage releases this tension, allowing circulation and healing. Deep-tissue massage, such as the Rolfing that helped Leon Fleisher, involves the manipulation of muscles and tendons deep within the body.

Other valuable relaxation measures include yoga, breathing exercises, and meditation. These are practices for the mind and body that can be done alone or in a group led by an instructor. They help balance the body's energies and enhance the healing process through increased blood flow and oxygenation. Yoga involves highly disciplined stretches that can benefit injured muscles and tendons. The RSI sufferer should let the yoga instructor know about her injury so that she is not pushed too far.

Another valuable practice is known as hydrotherapy, or water therapy. The usefulness of heat and ice has been mentioned, and hydrotherapy is the combination of both of these in alternating baths. The patient puts the injured part in a hot bath for three minutes, followed immediately by an ice bath for one minute, then repeats several times, finishing with the cold bath. The result is the enhancement of circulation to the injury in the hot bath alternated with the flushing of waste products of inflammation in the cold bath.

To prevent further injury, RSI patients must learn to stop risky activities or motions before they hurt.

Several vitamins have been indicated as helpful for healing RSIs, and some alternative practitioners recommend their use. Vitamins C and E and beta-carotene are all antioxidants. They help the healing of wounds by minimizing negative effects of free radicals (renegade molecules in the body that can damage cell membranes). Many people with CTS are deficient in vitamin $B_6$ and respond well to daily supplementation of the vitamin. It should only be taken under the supervision of a doctor. Too much $B_6$ can cause nerve damage. Perhaps the recent rise in occurrence of CTS parallels the increase in substances in our food and drugs, such as certain yellow dyes, that counteract vitamin $B_6$.[8]

Two botanical agents that can prove useful to RSI sufferers are turmeric and bromelain, both of which belong to the potent biologically active chemicals called bioflavonoids. Turmeric is an Asian spice long used in Indian and Chinese medicine for its anti-inflammatory properties and high vitamin C content. It is comparable in its effects to hydrocortisone. It is especially useful for acute cases of inflammation when the yellow pigment in the spice, called curcumin, is isolated. Bromelain, an enzyme from the pineapple plant, fights inflammation and breaks down proteins such as those found in scar tissue. It is especially valuable to RSI patients if they undergo surgery.[9] Turmeric and bromelain are readily available in health food stores or from naturopathic doctors or other alternative practitioners.

Other alternative therapies include chiropractic, which involves spinal manipulations to correct improper alignment.

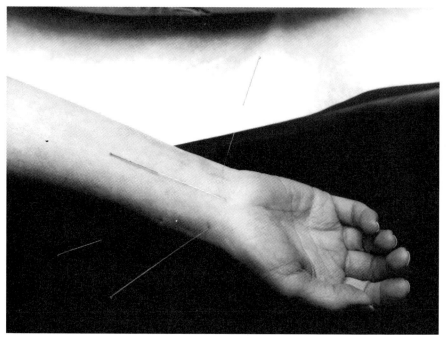

Acupuncture is a helpful alternative treatment for many RSI sufferers.

Chiropractors can be instrumental in eliminating from the body some of the imbalanced muscle strain that contributes to RSI.

Acupuncture, involving the stimulation of specific points with needles, can balance physical and energetic stresses and release soothing hormones called endorphins. This ancient Asian practice is one of the most successful treatments for RSIs and can result in complete recovery in a relatively short time.

Transcutaneous electrical nerve stimulation (TENS) involves placing electrodes on acupuncture points and introducing low-voltage electrical current to reduce pain. Alpha-stimulation is a similar treatment using even lower voltage. Low-energy laser treatments penetrate the skin and stimulate circulation in the underlying tissue, reducing inflammation and encouraging nerve regeneration. Just as ultrasound therapy can be combined with cortisone, it can also be combined with homeopathic creams for a similar result.

An individual alternative therapy may not work in every case, but these therapies should not be disregarded just because they are not condoned by all doctors. Most RSI patients who are in pain would go to any lengths to find relief, and these therapies can be powerful healing tools.

## Time and Patience

Rehabilitation is a long road that takes patience and courage to travel. It is critical during this healing time that patients take care of themselves in every way and not try to find shortcuts. Most healing occurs during sleep, so plenty of quality sleep is important. Patients must also eat a diet full of nutritious foods or take supplementary vitamins and minerals. Reducing the stresses of daily life, though it may be difficult, will allow the body to heal more readily. Patients should be aware of what causes them stress and work on eliminating the sources from their daily routine. Warm baths and supportive friends are always helpful.

# 7

# The Cost of Ignorance

**B**onnie felt a tingling in her right pinkie one day as she was typing at the computer. She worked for RCA, a record company, and spent many hours a day typing articles for advertising and publicity. She did not know about RSI and the tingling pinkie came as a surprise to her. Bonnie did what most people with a job and a deadline would do: She ignored her pinkie and kept on typing. Within a half hour, her whole right arm and hand were numb, making typing impossible. She could no longer ignore what her body was trying to tell her. Bonnie was injured by repetitive motions.[1]

In less than a month, Bonnie could not type at all. She could not open a doorknob. She could not even tie her shoes or get dressed without wincing in pain. Both of her arms were effectively disabled. Facing the fact that she had RSI was hard for Bonnie, as it would be for anyone. She would probably have to change professions and undergo months of rehabilitation, and even then her disability might be permanent. But what made things worse was that she got no support from her employer.[2]

Bonnie filed a worker's compensation claim, but RCA asserted that the injury was not work-related. They moved her into a smaller office and excluded her from meetings. She was given a 40 percent salary cut, with the option of accepting it or being fired. Instead of feeling acknowledged for her many hours of work, let alone that her work was dangerous to her health, Bonnie felt intimidated and harassed by her employer.[3] And Bonnie is not the only RSI sufferer who feels that way about her employer.

## The Injured Society

Society as a whole is damaged by its ignorance of RSI. If people put up with unsafe and unhealthy work environments and are injured as a result, society pays in the end through increased medical costs and social disruption.[4] The Occupational Safety and Health Administration (OSHA) estimates that RSI accounts for 60 percent of all workplace illnesses, costing employers $100 billion annually.[5] As more and more people spend considerable amounts of time at the computer, RSI rates may rise, and the costs may rise through the roof with them. Common awareness of RSI risks can slow the pace of injury.

OSHA has tried to institute regulations that would require more attention and awareness of RSI by employers. These regulations would identify and define RSI risk factors such as heavy lifting, working in cramped places, and using vibrating tools. They would also redefine high-risk jobs.

The proposed regulations have met strong resistance from business owners who complain that compliance would cost lots of money and change the way they operate. They feel unfairly judged, because beyond the fact of RSI's existence, there is little agreement over the scope or cause of them. Regulating something without a firm understanding of its cause seems premature especially if you run a business that will bear the brunt of the cost involved. Business executives worry that OSHA would make every job an RSI "waiting to happen."[6]

Meanwhile, businesses are being presented with lawsuits. More than two thousand suits have been filed in the United States against computer manufacturers by people who feel they were injured using their equipment.[7] Some RSI sufferers have filed suit under the Americans with Disabilities Act that requires companies to make "reasonable accommodations" for people injured on the job by repetitive motions. Unfortunately, these lawsuits cost businesses even more money. The expense from these lawsuits could have been avoided by the minimal cost of making jobs safe, in the first place.

## RSI at Work

A person with RSI faces many challenges at work. If he does not know about the risks of repetitive motions, he will not know to seek help before his symptoms get serious. Many people assume that their job activities, such as typing, are not

An awareness of the risk factors for RSI can help companies avoid injury to their employees.

strenuous and could not lead to injury. Others have a stubborn attitude about pain and deny the urgent messages from their bodies. Even if they do know about RSI, people may try to hide their symptoms so that they do not damage a good relationship with their employer. As Stephanie Barnes of the Association for Repetitive Motion Syndromes puts it, "They know that if they can't perform, there's always someone to take their job."[8]

Many employers have accepted the responsibilities of work-related RSI and have taken measures to accommodate the safety of their employees. After two RSI cases, MacWorld, a distributor of computer equipment, instituted mandatory breaks among its workers, invested fifty thousand dollars in adjustable ergonomic equipment, and hired a consultant to instruct workers on the proper use of the equipment. IBM began training its employees in the proper use of computer equipment in the early 1980s.[9] These companies set an example for others to follow.

Accepting their injuries is the first hurdle for workers. RSI sufferers may also have to educate other people at work about their condition. Employers may agree that the worker needs to take more breaks to avoid RSI, but they may also expect the same amount of work from them, making the benefit of the breaks negligible. Communication between the worker and his employer becomes very important at this point if they are to continue having a positive working relationship. A job that may have been stressful in the first place, contributing to the onset of RSI, can become even more stressful once the RSI sufferer tries to accommodate his injury.

Many people with RSI go through five stages of dealing with their injury: denial, panic, anger, depression, and mastery. Denial comes from ignorance about the RSI condition, fear of losing a job, or a false sense of security that things like this "won't happen to me." Panic comes when the reality of the injury looms and the sufferer imagines losing his job or maybe even family support. Anger and frustration are common emotions among RSI sufferers; they may become angry at their job, at their boss, at everyone who is skeptical, and even at their computer or tennis racquet. When depression overwhelms them, they may feel helpless, as if they cannot do anything to reverse the injury that has taken over their bodies. Finally, mastering RSI involves getting past the other stages and working to heal the injury and get on with life.[10]

The progression of emotions may be a positive growth experience. But growth may take months, even years, in an unsupportive environment. Many of the emotions felt during this period can have a negative effect on RSI, aggravating its symptoms. It is important for RSI sufferers to work through the emotions as quickly and effectively as possible. This can be aided by the support of a loving family, an attentive physician or therapist, the help of a friend, or the advice of a good counselor. There are certainly cases in which an enlightened employer makes the difference between a debilitating work-related injury and a speedy recovery.

# If You Know Someone Who Has RSI

- Ask before shaking his hand.
- Open doors for her.
- Help him carry things.
- Offer to help her do manual chores like shopping, cooking, and cleaning.
- Encourage him to seek help.

Many people with RSI find relief in support groups formed of other people with similar afflictions. Sometimes support groups are run by a professional, such as a psychotherapist or social worker, and sometimes they are run by the group members. From sharing their stories and hearing those of others, members gain inspiration, help with resolving work problems, and healing advice that may be unavailable from doctors.

## RSI at the Doctor's Office

Many doctors are aware of and sympathetic to RSI. The identification and definition of RSI is still relatively new, so doctors may not always be aware of the implications of RSI symptoms. Not all doctors have an intimate knowledge of workstation design or the risks of repetitive motion. Some doctors may tell patients to just use the other hand. Many cases are diagnosed as CTS when they are really tendinitis or deQuervain's disease. Some patients will see at least six specialists, rheumatologists, hand surgeons, neurologists, or orthopedists before they are properly diagnosed.[11]

One of the keys to healing RSI is finding the right doctor. He or she should be someone the patient can trust, because the patient will need the support of the doctor through her conflicts at work and at home. The right doctor will be the RSI patient's advocate through the range of emotions and societal reactions that she will experience. The right doctor will verify that she indeed has a serious injury.

# 8

# Stop the Repetition

**N**obody knows whether he or she is going to get RSI. Someone may be kneading bread one day and suddenly have shooting pains in the wrist. Or he might work for years as a meat packer or computer operator without a problem until the day he tries playing golf. Because RSI can be so sneaky and can take many months to treat, the best treatment is prevention. By eliminating as many risk factors as possible, even someone who does repetitive motions for a living can reduce the chances of getting RSI to close to zero.

Of course, some risk factors are difficult to change. If you want to be a cellist, you cannot avoid spending many hours reaching around your instrument. If you have a slight build or have inherited weak wrists, you will need to pay special attention to other risk factors that you can change. But whether repetitive motions are done at work or at home, everyone can benefit from taking a few simple precautions to prevent RSI. Most preventative measures involve resting, stretching, conditioning, or positioning your muscles to reduce straining them. Other measures have to do with the work environment and mental attitude.

# Resting

Working or playing without periodic breaks is a surefire way to get RSI. Rest allows your muscles to rejuvenate after a strain, giving them time to flush toxins out and get recharged with oxygen and nutrients. Most tasks automatically require some breaks, whether it is getting up to pull a file at an office or changing court sides in a tennis match. But if you are doing any one task for several hours a day, it can only benefit you to purposely take breaks of five to ten minutes every hour. You can be doing other related tasks, but give the muscles that perform your repetitive task a break.

# Exercise

Exercising can make your muscles more supple and strong and less likely to suffer a strain. But you can have too much of a good thing. If you perform a repetitive task at work, your forearms may already be suffering from overuse, so lifting weights to strengthen them can lead to further risk of injury unless it is done very carefully and under supervision. You will probably benefit more from strengthening your back and shoulders to take over more of the work.

The most important step in stopping RSI is to listen to your body, whether on the job or enjoying your favorite recreation.

Muscles work together: Some are stretched while others contract to perform a movement. Repetitive motions that can lead to RSI often involve an imbalance in this cooperation, with some muscles becoming too tight from overuse while others become stretched and weak. You may not notice this imbalance, but it is as unnatural and debilitating as pedaling a bicycle with one leg. For instance, someone who slouches over a computer all day has tight muscles in the chest and unconditioned muscles in the back, so it is the back that needs strengthening exercises.

Every case of conditioning is unique because of the muscles used for different tasks as well as people's distinct physical makeups. It helps to have the advice of an occupational therapist or someone else who knows about RSI to find the best specific strengthening exercises in each case. The proper training includes understanding the reasoning behind each exercise. This awareness can mean the difference between effective conditioning and doing boring, meaningless exercises.

## Stretching

The complement to exercising is stretching. In the case of the slouching computer worker, the chest muscles should be stretched in concert with strengthening the back. Stretching muscles releases tension built up within them and reduces the effects of strains. It promotes healing by bringing vital oxygen and nutrients to the muscle tissue. It can also free up binding scar tissue and sticky tendons that make movement difficult, adding to the risk of injury. Stretching is one of the best things you can do for yourself if you have any risk factors for RSI. It takes so little time there is no reason not to stretch.

An appropriate stretching regimen will include several stretches specific to the muscles and tendons that are overused in work or play. Many stretches can be done at work or school and are a constructive use of break time. They can be as simple as rotating your wrist with your hand in a fist, or they may involve props like a bench or desk on which to rest your hands. In every case the stretches are to be done slowly and steadily, without pushing too far or making jerky, bouncing motions. Tendons are like hard taffy; they are not soft enough to stretch quickly. If a stretch is painful, then you are only adding to the potential of injury. The key is finding the "stretch point" for each exercise, when you can feel the first subtle ache of easing tendons. The ache should disappear in a few seconds. If you find the stretch point and work with it so that you can stretch farther and farther each time, your risks of RSI will diminish. Like chewing hard taffy, stretching gets easier with time and repetition.

## Posture

Your body was designed to move—to chase woolly mammoths with spears and run away from saber-toothed tigers—so standing on an assembly line, twisting screws, comes as a strain. Sitting in a chair, twiddling a keyboard, is even worse, no matter how ergonomically designed or cushy the chair is. The continuous strain on your back and other body parts is

Many of the motions that we take for granted, even find relaxing, can contribute to RSI.

hard for your body to endure even in the best circumstances. But when you add cramped working quarters, bad lighting, poor tool design, bad posture, and improper technique to that, you have a recipe for disaster. It may not be as immediate as a saber-toothed tiger, but it is nearly as dangerous.

Well-aligned standing posture is the foundation for minimizing the risk of RSI. When your body is straight, the vertebrae are stacked like blocks and the muscles are working in balance, not fighting gravity. Nerves and blood vessels run their course without binding or pinching. But the way you hold yourself is a habit that begins very early in life, and bad posture is consequently difficult to change. Bad posture may reflect psychological issues, such as low self-esteem or self-consciousness, that require even more effort to address. Bad posture and its emotional associations may not be a strain itself until it is combined with other risk factors, such as typing on a keyboard in a stressful work environment or slicing open fish all day. In such a case posture can contribute to job-related stress as well as reflect it.[1]

That is not to say you need to sit or stand as straight as a board at your job. Trying to keep your back straight can put as much strain on your muscles as slouching. Shifting positions now and then is actually better than any one position, because it keeps your muscles loose and uses different ones at different times. Standing up to do other tasks is helpful. Even slouching once in a while is no felony, as long as you avoid doing it for four hours straight. Constructive fidgeting, never staying in one position too long, is the best practice to follow. Many people find practices like yoga helpful in improving their posture. There are also practitioners such as chiropractors who may be able to manipulate your alignment toward better posture.

## Positioning

The other half of good posture is good positioning and technique, whether it is how you hold your hands over a keyboard or how you swing a hammer. Often these movements include habits that you acquired when you first started doing them and are difficult to notice because they are so familiar. For an easy example, fold your arms across your chest. Now do it again with the opposite arm on top, and see how awkward and unnatural it feels. The same goes for how you fold your hands, hold a phone, cast a fishing rod, drive a car, or handle a power drill. Habits are inevitable, but where you run into trouble is where it involves tightening certain muscles to hold joints still, or the imbalanced use of muscles. These muscles are then vulnerable to RSI.

Every joint has a neutral position in which each muscle and tendon is at a medium length, neither contracted or extended too far. This position is where your muscles are most efficient, so it requires less force to perform motions and causes less fatigue and irritation. The goal of proper positioning at work or play is to have each joint operating at or near that neutral position. Wrists should be straight, not bent up or down or to either side. Elbows should be bent at 90 degrees. Fingers and thumbs should be relaxed and slightly bent, not straining to squeeze or stretch. The same principles apply if you are working on a keyboard or butchering a side of beef. The more you can work from the neutral positions, the safer your work or play can be.

## Ergonomics

Of course, some aspects of positioning are beyond your control. If you are four feet tall and work at an assembly-line bench that is designed for someone six feet tall, you will be forced into some uncomfortable and far-from-neutral positions. Position can be affected by the height of the table or chair, the shape and design of tools, and the lighting or space in which you are required to work. Ergonomics is the study of how these elements of workstation design interact with the movements of the human body.

The object of ergonomics is to fit the task to the person, instead of vice versa. Chairs can be adjusted to be comfortable and give firm back support to avoid slouching, with the feet resting flat on the floor and the knees slightly lower than the hips. If they have armrests, they should be adjusted to a half inch lower than the forearm when working to avoid shrugging or slouching. Desks or tables should be elbow height so that the elbow can rest in neutral position. Keyboards should not be tilted up, requiring the wrists to tip up, and mouse pads should be within reach at a neutral position. Computer monitors or other visual tools should be at eye level and straight ahead, not requiring any twisting of the neck. Every element of the work involved should be custom fitted to the person

91

who will be performing it. This way, he can maintain neutral positioning and avoid working extra against gravity.

Many useful tools have been developed out of the study of ergonomics that can make work easier and safer. Adjustable chairs, ergonomic keyboards, telephone headsets, and voice-activated computers can all make a significant difference in the RSI risk factors encountered at work. One of the simplest solutions is a pen expander, which makes pens fatter and less of a strain to write with. Wrist rests, on the other hand, are not so helpful. Many people believe that by using a padded wrist rest when they type they are avoiding RSI. Actually this is no better than resting their hands on the table while they type. It still requires the hands to do all the stretching and rapid movements without the aid of the stronger arms and upper body. Wrist rests are fine to rest their hands on when they are *not* typing, but proper typing position requires hands to hover over the keys, supported by the arms.[2]

In the end, all the ergonomic furniture and fancy gee-whiz gimmicks in the world will not make a difference if bad technique continues. For instance, a steadfast sloucher can still manage to slouch in a state-of-the-art adjustable chair. An ergonomic keyboard is useless if the operator rests his hands on the desk anyway. Finding the right equipment starts with knowing your body and knowing what it feels like to move correctly and with good posture. Once you know what this feels like, then choosing and adjusting the right equipment will come easily.[3]

# The Mind-Body Connection[4]

Your state of mind is intimately related to how your body moves and acts. When a person is tense, her muscles become tight and more vulnerable to injury. Try this experiment: Scrunch your nose as tightly as you can and hold it that way. Then try to walk around. Now relax your nose and walk around again. Most people find that the added tension affects their feet. Did you? Experiment with other parts of your body.

## Psychological Aspects

Many people have a high risk of RSI simply because of the environment in which they work or play, or the mental attitude they bring with them. Even something as relaxing as a game of golf can be stressful if you get angry with yourself when you lob the ball into the pond: Your muscles tighten, your joints stiffen, and your body is more susceptible to injury. Some people who work with computers are terrified of them, adding a good deal of stress to their work. Workplaces can be smelly, loud, or involve tight schedules or cranky bosses. Changing your work environment is not easy, but changing your own reaction to the environment is possible through stress management. This can involve yoga, guided relaxation exercises, or even taking a walk or a hot bath at the end of the day.

Many people go through their lives focusing their attention on desires, like what they want for dinner, what kind of car they want, whom they want to date, where they want to live, what job they want to do. When your mind is preoccupied with such external things, it is easy to ignore what is going on inside your body. A little bit of attention to your body can go a long way toward preventing RSI. Taking a few seconds now and then to adjust muscles that are tense or overly stretched, to feel whether your breathing is relaxed and full, to shift your weight so that your posture is balanced and easy may go a long way toward prevention. If you pay attention to what is good for your body, you can act out of common sense.[5]

# 9

# The Future of RSI

**W**e are in the midst of an RSI epidemic. Whether the epidemic grows with future generations will depend on the concerted efforts of both doctors and their patients to learn more about its risk and how to prevent it. Doctors will need to recognize and accurately diagnose the different forms of RSI and to recommend comprehensive rehabilitation plans to nip them in the bud. Patients will have to be more aware of repetitive motions that they use in their daily lives and how to minimize the risks associated with them. Tennis players and trombone players alike must learn to take breaks, stretch and condition their bodies with care, and improve their posture and positioning to reduce strains to their muscles.

# The Future of Work

The most important changes to stem the rising rate of RSI are modifications in the workplace. More and more employers are recognizing that their workers' health is more important than the speed with which they assemble a part or type a page. Personnel-focused work practices include providing a stress-free environment with adequate lighting and without crowding or loud sounds. It involves training employees to work safely and allowing the time and motivation to learn proper technique. It means finding jobs that fit each one's personal limits. Companies of the future will accept that short-term gains are not worth the long-term risks in employee health and productivity.

Any job can be surveyed for its risk of RSI by using a process called work-methods analysis. Each motion that the job entails is tallied on a list, including ones that contribute to strain, such as reaching, grasping, and twisting. Work space and design, tool design, and the postures necessary to complete a task all need critical analysis. Tasks that involve excessive strain or repetitive movements should be adjusted for the sake of the worker. Jobs should not require workers to exert more than 30 percent of their maximum force in a prolonged or repetitive way or for more than 50 percent of the time. Variety should be included in a day's tasks, and pauses or breaks should be encouraged.[1] These standards will be the hallmark of successful businesses in the future.

Employers of the future will monitor the rate of RSI cases associated with work tasks in order to prevent them. This could be accomplished by reviewing available records, surveying workers, or analyzing the ergonomics of each job. In some companies today, a rate of six RSI cases per 200,000 work hours (for instance, 100 workers working 2,000 hours, or one year of full-time work) is considered acceptable.[2] But if you are one of those six people, you may not agree.

## The Future Is Now

Many companies have already realized that worker safety is cost-effective. In the long run, greater comfort and attention

# The Future of Job Pressure

Many jobs have aspects that make the company more productive; but these same aspects also make the jobs more stressful and injury-prone. These include

- Incentives: rewards for working harder or faster or for putting in more overtime
- Monitoring: computer monitoring of employees' pace and productivity, increasing the level of paranoia and stress
- Impersonal atmosphere: making the job more boring, more isolating
- Hierarchies: more and more bosses lead to personal devaluation and job dissatisfaction

to posture and position will reduce fatigue and improve the performance of their workers. They have taken steps toward a future in which RSI will be uncommon. United States businesses now spend 2 billion dollars a year on ergonomic furniture—desks, chairs, and other workstation accessories. The number of RSI cases reported in the workplace has been responding to this awareness and has been falling since 1994.[3] The future course of RSI depends on how many other companies follow the examples of their more aware colleagues.

The future of RSI is, quite literally, in your hands. The next generation of workers and players will determine whether

The future of RSI rests largely on the habits and practices of today's young people, especially the millions that are using computers.

RSI becomes a once-feared disease of a bygone century, like smallpox or bubonic plague, or an integral epidemic of the modern age. If people are to continue with the trend of mechanization and computerization that has brought RSI to the forefront, it will be important for all individuals to realize and respect the physical limitations of their own bodies.

# Q & A

**Q.** How is carpal tunnel syndrome different from repetitive strain injury?

**A.** CTS is one form of repetitive strain injury. It is often confused with other types of RSIs because it is the most commonly recognized form.

**Q.** Why should I worry about RSI if it mostly affects adults?

**A.** It mostly affects adults with poor posture or improper physical conditioning, both of which stem from habits that you can adjust more easily when you are young. Now is the best time to start good habits.

**Q.** Should I not take a job if it requires me to do repetitive motions?

**A.** No. Any job can be safe, as long as precautions are taken that the workstation, tools, and workload allow for correct posture and positioning and sufficient time for breaks.

**Q.** If my mother has carpal tunnel syndrome, does that mean I will get it one day?

**A.** No. There may be factors in your genetic makeup, such as a slight build, that can contribute to RSI, but your mother had other nongenetic factors in her habits or work that led to her injury.

**Q.** My brother was diagnosed with tendinitis. Should he start lifting weights to strengthen his muscles so that he does not strain his tendons any more?

**A.** Not right away. He will want to recondition his muscles, but lifting weights after an injury should only be done gradually and under the supervision of a physical therapist, or he will risk further damage to the tendons.

**Q.** My hands tingle when I ride my bicycle. Should I wear padded gloves?

**A.** Yes, and you may also try tilting your bike seat back and shifting your hand position more often. The tingling could be resulting from a compressed nerve or from lack of circulation, either of which could contribute to an RSI.

**Q.** Am I safe from RSI if I type on an ergonomic keyboard?

**A.** No. Ergonomic equipment is a great improvement, but it does not replace proper posture. It is important to support the hands with the upper arms and body.

**Q.** My grandmother started getting aches in her elbows when she swept, but her doctor told her she was just getting old. Should she ask someone else?

**A.** Yes. She should find a doctor who is aware of and sympathetic to RSI.

**Q.** How can I raise more awareness of RSI at school?

**A.** Hang a poster of healthful keyboard habits in the computer area; encourage the computer teacher to stress proper keyboard technique; invite an RSI sufferer to visit the school and talk to your class.

**Q.** Did people never used to get RSI?

**A.** People who performed repetitive motions, such as musicians or carpenters, have always suffered from RSI, although it only received that name in recent years. The computer age and the huge number of people now using computers for work and play has made RSI more common than it ever was.

# RSI Timeline

1713—Bernardino Ramazzini, the father of occupational medicine, identified that some positions and postures used at work can gradually lead to serious injury.

1873—Remington Arms Company introduced the first typewriter with familiar *QWERTY* keyboard.

1888—Dr. W. R. Gowers observed that writer's cramp can be prevented by writing from the shoulder rather than the wrist.

1911—Scientific management, introduced by Frederick Taylor, encouraged businesses to increase production by quickening pace and reducing workers to menial, repetitive tasks.

1913—Transverse carpal ligament at the base of the palm first implicated in compression of median nerve, to be referred to later as carpal tunnel syndrome.

1946—First published results of surgery on ligament to alleviate symptoms of median nerve compression.

1952—Phalen first described and named carpal tunnel syndrome.

1972—Bureau of Labor Statistics classifies RSI as an illness.

1980s—Repetitive strain injuries first recognized as a group of related conditions, and so named.

**1981**—IBM introduced the first personal computer.

**1985**—National Institute for Occupational Safety and Health proposed a national strategy for preventing RSI in the workplace.

**1990**—RSI rates in computer-intensive industries rose ten times in five years.

**1992**—The Americans with Disabilities Act enacted to protect the rights of workers with disabilities, including RSI.

**2000**—Three quarters of all jobs will require using a computer.

# For More Information

American Academy of Orthopaedic Surgeons
6300 N. River Road
Rosemont, IL 60018-4262
(800) 346-AAOS

American Occupational Therapy Association
4720 Montgomery Lane
Bethesda, MD 20814-34205
(301) 652-2682

Canadian Centre for Occupational Health and Safety
250 Main Street East
Hamilton, Ontario, Canada
L8N 1H6

Carpal Tunnel Syndrome/RSI Association
P.O. Box 514
Santa Rosa, CA 95402

Cumulative Trauma Disorder Resource Network (CTDRN)
2013 Princeton Court
Los Banos, CA 93635
(209) 826-8443

National Institute of Arthritis and Musculoskeletal and Skin
Diseases
National Institutes of Health
Bethesda, MD 20892-2350
(301) 496-8188

**National Institute of Occupational Safety and Health (NIOSH)**
Technical Information Center
4676 Columbia Parkway
Cincinnati, OH 45226
(800) 35NIOSH

**Occupational Safety and Health Administration**
U.S. Department of Labor
200 Constitution Avenue
Washington, DC 20210
(202) 523-1452

**Time Out for Windows**
(Online ergonomic exercises by S. Systems Corp.)
5777 West Century Boulevard, Suite 575
Los Angeles, California, 90045
(310) 641-3260

# Internet Addresses

American Academy of Orthopaedic Surgeons. "AAOS On-Line." November 8, 1999. <http://www.aaos.org>

Canadian Centre for Occupational Health and Safety. "Welcome to CCOHS." n.d. <http://www.ccohs.ca>

Center for Workplace Health. "CTDNews Online." November 1999. <http://www.CTDnews.com>

CTD Resource Network, Inc. "Typing Injury FAQ: The RSI Community Online Resource." October 7, 1999. <http://www.tifaq.com>

Marxhausen, Paul. "Computer Related Repetitive Strain Injury." 1996. <http://engr-www.unl.edu/ee/eeshop/rsi.html>

Mayo Clinic. "Overuse Strain Injury: Progressive Conditions Respond to Simple Care." 1999. <http://www.mayohealth.org/mayo/9510/htm/hotli_sb.htm>

National Institute of Arthritis and Musculoskeletal and Skin Diseases, National Institutes of Health. "NIAMS." *NIH Homepage.* n.d. <http://www.nih.gov/niams>

The Nemours Foundation. "Computers Can Be A Real Pain!" *Kid Health.org.* 1999. <http://www.kidshealth.org/kid/watch/k_ergonomics.html>

Occupational Safety and Health Administration. "OSHA Homepage." November 22, 1999. <http://www.osha.gov>

# Chapter Notes

## Chapter 1. The Disease of Monotony

1. Mary Lord, "Is Your Mouse a Trap?" *US News & World Report*, March 31, 1997, p. 76.

2. Vern Putz-Anderson, ed., *Cumulative Trauma Disorders* (Bristol, Pa.: Taylor & Francis, 1994), p. 3.

3. Emil Pascarelli and Deborah Quilter, *Repetitive Strain Injury* (New York: John Wiley & Sons, 1994), p. 50.

4. Lord, p. 76.

5. Putz-Anderson, p. 6.

6. Pascarelli and Quilter, p. 3.

7. Philip Elmer-DeWitt and Janice M. Horowitz, "A Royal Pain in the Wrist," *Time*, October 24, 1996, p. 60.

## Chapter 2. Birth of an Illness

1. Vern Putz-Anderson, ed., *Cumulative Trauma Disorders* (Bristol, Pa.: Taylor & Francis, 1994), p. 1.

2. Richard Norris, *The Musicians Survival Manual* (St. Louis, Mo.: MMB Music), p. 1.

3. Putz-Anderson, p. 1.

4. Ibid., p. 24.

5. Emil Pascarelli and Deborah Quilter, *Repetitive Strain Injury* (New York: John Wiley & Sons, 1994), pp. 1–2.

6. Philip Elmer-DeWitt and Janice M. Horowitz, "A Royal Pain in the Wrist," *Time*, October 24, 1994, p. 60.

7. Mary Lord, "Is Your Mouse a Trap?" *US News & World Report*, March 31, 1997, p. 76.

8. Pascarelli and Quilter, p. vii.

9. Ibid., p. 9.

10. Putz-Anderson, p. 144.

11. Pascarelli and Quilter, p. 3.

## Chapter 3. The Slowest Injury

1. Author's interview with Jane, September 28, 1998.

2. Ben E. Benjamin, *Listen to Your Pain* (New York: Penguin Books, 1984), p. 6.

3. Vern Putz-Anderson, ed., *Cumulative Trauma Disorders* (Bristol, Pa.: Taylor & Francis, 1994), p. 12.

4. Philip Elmer-DeWitt and Janice M. Horowitz, "A Royal Pain in the Wrist," *Time*, October 24, 1994, p. 60.

5. Putz-Anderson, p. 16.

6. Marko Pecina, Jelina Krmpotic-Nemanic, and Andrew Markiewitz, *Tunnel Syndromes: Peripheral Nerve Compression*, 2nd ed. (Boca Raton, Fla.: CRC Press, 1997), p. 122.

7. Ibid.

8. Interview with Jane.

## Chapter 4. Repetition as a Way of Life

1. Susan Reed, "Once More, With Feeling," *People Weekly*, February 26, 1996, p. 85.

2. Ibid.

3. Emil Pascarelli and Deborah Quilter, *Repetitive Strain Injury* (New York: John Wiley & Sons, 1994), p. 33.

4. Paul Linden, *Compute in Comfort* (Upper Saddle River, N.J.: Prentice Hall, 1995), p. 24.

5. Sharon J. Butler, *Conquering Carpal Tunnel Syndrome and Other Repetitive Strain Injuries* (Berwyn, Pa.: Advanced Press, 1995), pp. 33–36, 39.

## Chapter 5. Finding the Pain

1. Susan Reed, "Once More, With Feeling," *People Weekly*, February 26, 1996, p. 85.

2. Emil Pascarelli and Deborah Quilter, *Repetitive Strain Injury* (New York: John Wiley & Sons, 1994), p. 49.

3. Marko Pecina, Jelina Krmpotic-Nemanic, and Andrew Markiewitz, *Tunnel Syndromes: Peripheral Nerve Compression*, 2nd ed. (Boca Raton, Fla.: CRC Press, 1997), p. 19.

4. CTD News On-line, July 1996 Summary, Center for Workplace Health Information, <http://www.CTDnews.com/numbers.htm> (May 1, 1998).

## Chapter 6. Healing the Strain

1. Richard Norris, *The Musicians Survival Manual* (St. Louis, Mo.: MMB Music, 1993), p. 17.

2. Emil Pascarelli and Deborah Quilter, *Repetitive Strain Injury* (New York: John Wiley & Sons, 1994), p. 75.

3. Vern Putz-Anderson, ed., *Cumulative Trauma Disorders* (Bristol, Pa.: Taylor & Francis, 1994), p. 124.

4. Ben E. Benjamin, *Listen to Your Pain* (New York: Penguin Books, 1984), p. 35.

5. Marko Pecina, Jelina Krmpotic-Nemanic, and Andrew Markiewitz, *Tunnel Syndromes: Peripheral Nerve Compression*, 2nd ed. (Boca Raton, Fla.: CRC Press, 1997), p. 11.

6. Ibid., p. 12.

7. Ibid., pp. 11–12.

8. Michael Murray and Joseph Pizzorno, *Encyclopedia of Natural Medicine* (Rocklin, Calif.: Prima Publishing, 1991), p. 190.

9. Ibid., pp. 190–191.

## Chapter 7. The Cost of Ignorance

1. Philip Elmer-DeWitt and Janice M. Horowitz, "A Royal Pain in the Wrist," *Time*, October 24, 1994, p. 60.

2. Ibid.

3. Ibid.

4. Paul Linden, *Compute in Comfort* (Upper Saddle River, N.J.: Prentice Hall, 1995), p. 21.

5. Michael Meyer, "A Pain for Business," *Newsweek*, June 26, 1995, p. 42.

6. Ibid.

7. Elmer-DeWitt and Horowitz, p. 60.

8. Ibid., p. 61.

9. Ibid., p. 62.

10. Emil Pascarelli and Deborah Quilter, *Repetitive Strain Injury* (New York: John Wiley & Sons, 1994), pp. 134–137.

11. Ibid., p. 41.

## Chapter 8. Stop the Repetition

1. Paul Linden, *Compute in Comfort* (Upper Saddle River, N.J.: Prentice Hall, 1995), p. 20.

2. Emil Pascarelli and Deborah Quilter, *Repetitive Strain Injury* (New York: John Wiley & Sons, 1994), p. 157.

3. Linden, p. 4.

4. Ibid., p. 13.

5. Ibid., p. 12.

## Chapter 9. The Future of RSI

1. Vern Putz-Anderson, ed., *Cumulative Trauma Disorders* (Bristol, Pa.: Taylor & Francis, 1994), p. 79.

2. Ibid., p. 39.

3. CTD News On-line, July 1996 Summary, Center for Workplace Health Information, <http://www.CTDnews.com/numbers.htm>. (May 1, 1998).

# Glossary

**activity of daily living (ADL)**—A common motion such as brushing hair or turning the faucet, often useful in diagnosing RSI.

**acupuncture**—Ancient Asian healing art that involves inserting long needles into the body at specific points.

**analgesic**—Any drug that numbs the pain associated with RSI without causing unconsciousness.

**angiogram**—A diagnostic tool for detecting the constriction of a blood vessel: A die is injected into the bloodstream and the vessels are photographed with X rays.

**anti-inflammatory**—Any drug that depresses the swelling associated with injury, easing symptoms of RSI but at times interfering with the healing process.

**atrophy**—A wasting away of part of the body.

**biofeedback**—A tool for improving safe technique, by which the force applied to muscles during an activity is electrically detected and displayed on a computer.

**carpal tunnel syndrome (CTS)**—An RSI of the wrist, resulting from the compression of the median nerve by neighboring tendons as they pass under a tight ligament.

**clacker**—Someone who bangs the computer keyboard hard, making his or her hands and arms vulnerable to injury.

**computed tomography (CT)**—A diagnostic scanning tool that produces detailed three-dimensional images of the bony anatomy of the body.

**connective tissue**—Any of several expansive tissues made of cells floating in a matrix, including blood, bone, cartilage, tendons, and ligaments.

**cubital tunnel syndrome**—Compression of the ulnar nerve, which runs to the pinkie finger, as it passes through a tight spot under the elbow.

**cumulative trauma**—Any bodily injury resulting from the additive effects of some injurious activity repeated many times.

**deconditioned**—Describes muscles that are out of shape, making them tight, rigid, and vulnerable to injury.

**deep-tissue massage**—Any therapy that involves the manipulation of muscles and tendons deep within the body.

**deQuervain's disease**—Inflammation of the tendon and synovium at the base of the thumb near the wrist.

**dermatome**—A body area originating from one of the original thirty-two segments that make up an embryo; helpful in determining the range of referred pain.

**dorsiflexion**—The injurious wrist position found in many typists in which the hand is rotated up in the "stop" position.

**dynamic action**—Any exertion of the muscles that requires tensing and relaxing in sequence, helping pump blood in and out of the muscle tissue.

**electrodiagnostic testing**—Using electrical impulses to test the health of nerves, which are often damaged in RSI.

**electromyography (EMG)**—A diagnostic tool for detecting injuries to nerves by testing for electrical impulses in the muscles they activate.

**endoscopic surgery**—Surgery performed through a small incision, using a tiny fiber-optic tube, sometimes performed on patients with carpal tunnel syndrome.

**ergonomics**—The study of how tools and workstations most effectively fit the dimensions and movements of the human body.

**extensor**—A muscle that extends a body part, such as the one on the top of the forearm that controls the straightening of the fingers.

**extensor tendinitis**—Inflammation of the tendon that connects the extensor muscle on top of the forearm to the finger bones.

**flexor**—A muscle that bends a body part, such as the muscle under the forearm that controls the bending of the fingers.

**flexor tendinitis**—Inflammation of the tendon that connects the flexor muscle under the forearm to the finger bones.

**hydrocortisone**—A steroid hormone derivative sometimes injected into injured body parts to reduce inflammation.

**hydrotherapy**—Therapy involving the alternation of hot and cold baths, useful for providing circulation to injured body parts.

**inflammation**—A physical reaction to an injury that involves increased blood flow and muscle stiffness and swelling; it helps in the healing process.

lateral epicondylitis—Inflammation of the tendon that connects the extensor muscle in the forearm to the outside of the elbow; also called tennis elbow.

ligament—A tough, inelastic connective tissue usually connecting bone to bone; sometimes responsible for restricting tissues and creating tunnel syndromes.

magnetic resonance imaging (MRI)—A diagnostic scanning technique used to depict detailed images of internal soft anatomy, including damage to tendons involved in RSI.

medial epicondylitis—Inflammation of the tendon that connects the flexor muscle under the forearm to the inside of the elbow; also called golfer's elbow.

median nerve—The nerve that runs under the wrist to the thumb and first three fingers; compressed in carpal tunnel syndrome.

muscle—A soft elastic tissue responsible for the movement of bones; susceptible to strain if not properly conditioned and stretched.

muscle relaxant—Any drug that relaxes the tension in muscles, sometimes speeding the healing process.

musculoskeletal system—The network of bones, muscles, and related tissues that support the body and allow it to move.

nerve—A long, branching, fibrous tissue responsible for transmitting impulses to and from the brain; vulnerable to injury from compression by neighboring tissues.

nerve conduction velocity (NCV)—A diagnostic test of nerve function in which an electrical impulse is passed through a nerve so that the speed of conduction can be detected.

**neurovascular disorder**—A disorder that involves the compression of nerves as well as the interruption of normal blood circulation.

**neutral position**—The position of the arms or other body parts in which the muscles controlling them are neither too far contracted nor extended, where they are most efficient and less likely to strain.

**Occupational Safety and Health Administration (OSHA)**—Federal agency that regulates the safety and health rules for business and industry.

**occupational therapy**—Training and exercises that allow a worker to perform his tasks without risk of RSI.

**pain management**—The first step in recovery from RSI; involves rest, adaptation of activities of daily living, heat and cold applications, and drug therapy.

**positioning**—The angle of the arms and head when performing a task, which must be unstrained and balanced to avoid RSI.

**posture**—The alignment of the body in a sitting or standing position, which must be balanced to avoid RSI.

**proliferant**—Any drug that promotes the production of new tissue; used in RSI patients to regenerate injured tendons.

**radial tunnel syndrome**—Compression of the radial nerve in the forearm by neighboring tissues.

**Raynaud's phenomenon**—Constriction of blood vessels in the fingers, either from sensitivity to cold, forceful gripping, or using vibrating tools; also called white finger.

**reconditioning**—The strengthening of muscles to prevent further injury.

**referred pain**—A pain that occurs somewhere away from the site of injury, often misleading diagnosis.

**rehabilitation**—The slow, gradual exercising of injured parts to restore normal strength and flexibility.

**repetitive strain injury (RSI)**—Any injury to muscle, tendon, or nerve tissue resulting from the cumulative effect of repetitive motions combined with other risk factors.

**risk factor**—Any circumstance that can contribute to an RSI, such as genetic predisposition, posture and positioning, or stress.

**splinting**—The restriction of movement of a body part affected by RSI, such as the wrist, to prevent further injury.

**static action**—Any exertion of the muscles that requires continual tension, which does not allow blood to pump freely in and out of the muscle tissue.

**stenosing tenosynovitis**—Progressive constriction and hardening of the synovium, making movement of the tendon inside it difficult.

**stress**—A physiological response to the environment that involves increased heart rate, higher blood pressure, and muscle tension that can contribute to RSI.

**stress management**—The use of exercise, yoga, or other techniques to help reduce the negative effects of stress.

**stretch point**—The point during a muscle stretch when the first subtle ache of stretching tissues can be felt; the healthiest point to stretch to and injurious to stretch beyond.

**synovial fluid**—The lubricating material that allows a tendon to glide freely through the synovium.

**synovium**—A sheath that protects and lubricates a tendon as it passes through tight spots or corners; also called synovial sheath.

**tarsal tunnel syndrome**—Compression of the posterior tibial nerve as it runs through the ankle on the way to the foot.

**tendinitis**—Inflammation of a tendon caused by a tiny tear or by friction against neighboring tissues.

**tendon**—A tough, fibrous connective tissue forming the inelastic connection between muscles and bones; susceptible to tearing or inflammation if muscles are worked past their limits.

**tenosynovitis**—Inflammation of the synovial sheath in response to irritation of the tendon it contains.

**thoracic outlet syndrome (TOS)**—Compression of nerves and blood vessels as they pass through the shoulder area, usually by muscles in the neck.

**transcutaneous electrical nerve stimulation (TENS)**—The application of low-voltage electrical current at acupuncture points to reduce pain.

**trigger finger**—An extreme case of inflammation and tightening in the synovial sheath of a finger tendon, creating jerky motions or inability to straighten the finger; also called stenosing tenosynovitis crepitans.

**tunnel syndrome**—Any condition in which the inflammation or constriction of neighboring tissues causes compression and potential injury of a nerve.

**ulnar deviation**—The injurious wrist position found in many typists in which the hand is bent to the outside to line up with the keys.

**ulnar tunnel syndrome**—Compression of the ulnar nerve in the wrist that goes to the pinkie finger.

**ultrasound therapy**—The projection of high-frequency sound waves into internal body parts to alleviate some of the causes and symptoms of RSI.

**upper body exerciser (UBE)**—An exercise tool for reconditioning the muscles of the arm; it looks like a bicycle for the hands.

**work-methods analysis**—The study of how work tasks are performed in order to improve their efficiency and safety.

**X ray**—A diagnostic tool that involves passing radiation through an injured part; it is used to eliminate many other conditions that are not RSI.

# Further Reading

## Books

Butler, Sharon J. *Conquering Carpal Tunnel Syndrome and other Repetitive Strain Injuries.* Berwyn, Pa.: Advanced Press, 1995.

Gordon, Stephen L., Sidney Blair, and Lawrence Fine. *Repetitive Motion Disorders of the Upper Extremities.* Rosemont, Ill.: American Academy of Orthopaedic Surgeons, 1995.

Lieberman, Julie Lyonn. *You Are Your Instrument: The Definitive Musician's Guide to Practice and Performances.* New York: Huiksi Music, 1991.

Linden, Paul. *Compute in Comfort.* Upper Saddle River, N.J.: Prentice Hall, 1995.

Montgomery, Kate. *Carpal Tunnel Syndrome: Prevention and Treatment.* San Diego: Sports Touch Publishing, 1994.

Norris, Richard. *The Musicians Survival Manual.* St. Louis, Mo.: MMB Music, 1993.

Pascarelli, Emil, and Deborah Quilter. *Repetitive Strain Injury: A Computer User's Guide.* New York: John Wiley & Sons, Inc., 1994.

Putz-Anderson, Vern, ed. *Cumulative Trauma Disorders: A Manual for Musculoskeletal Diseases of the Upper Limbs.* Bristol, Pa.: Taylor and Francis, 1994.

## Articles

DeMont, John. "A Pain in the Wrist." *Maclean's*, November 21, 1994, pp. 58–59.

Dreher, Nancy. "Are You Programmed for High-tech Harm?" *Current Health*, March 2, 1995, pp. 13–15.

Elmer-DeWitt, Philip, and Janice M. Horowitz. "A Royal Pain in the Wrist." *Time*, October 24, 1994, pp. 60–62.

Gibbs, Jerry. "Cast Off the Pain." *Outdoor Life*, October 1995, pp. 32–33.

Lord, Mary. "Is Your Mouse a Trap?" *U.S. News & World Report*, March 31, 1997, pp. 76–77.

Meyer, Michael. "A Pain for Business." *Newsweek*, June 26, 1995, p. 42.

Munson, Marty. "End of the Tunnel." *Prevention*, March 1995, pp. 22–23.

Reed, Susan. "Once More, With Feeling." *People*, February 26, 1996, pp. 85–87.

Spilner, Maggie. "Stop Wear-and-Tear Injuries Now." *Prevention*, October 1994, pp. 126–128.

Stocker, Sharon. "Wave Away Hand Pain." *Prevention*, November 1996, pp. 116–117.

# Index

## A
activities of daily living (ADLs), 52, 60
acupuncture, 73
alternative therapies, 69–71, 73
analgesics, 62
anti-inflammatories, 62, 71

## B
Bilic's pressure test, 55

## C
carpal tunnel syndrome (CTS), 11, 22, 31–32, 52, 54, 55, 56, 63, 64, 65, 71, 82
cervical radiculopathy, 27
chiropractic care, 71, 73, 90
computer users, 11, 17–19, 28, 29, 35, 40, 45–47
connective tissues, 23, 26, 51
cortisone, 22, 63
cubital tunnel syndrome, 27, 32

## D
deep tissue massage. See Rolfing.
deQuervain's disease, 30, 54, 55, 65, 82
dermatomes, 24
distal ulnar neuropathy, 27
drug therapy, 62
dynamic action, 43

## E
electrodiagnostic tests, 56–57
emotional factors, 48–49, 80, 82, 89
ergonomics, 87, 91–92, 97, 98
exercise, 68, 84, 86

## F
Finkelstein's sign, 54
Fleisher, Leon, 37–38, 51–52

## G
genetics, 40
golfer's elbow, 10, 28

## H
habits, 40, 53
health, 40–41
heat, 59, 60
hydrocortisone, 63
hydrotherapy, 70

## I
inflammation, 26, 27, 31, 32, 58, 59, 60, 62, 63, 66, 70, 71, 73

## J
job-related injuries, 12, 20, 79

## L
lateral epicondylitis, 28. See also tennis elbow.

## M
massage, 59, 69
medial epicondylitis, 28. See also golfer's elbow.
muscle
    atrophy, 65
    conditioning, 13, 39, 86
    deconditioning, 47
    reconditioning, 66, 68
    relaxants, 62
    strain, 25
musculoskeletal system, 25

## N
National Institute for Occupational Safety and Health, 19
nerve conduction velocity, 56
nerve disorders, 30–32
neurovascular disorders, 34–35
numbness, 22, 30, 31, 34, 35, 75

## O
Occupational Safety and Health Administration (OSHA), 57, 76, 77
occupational therapy, 60, 66, 68–69, 86

127